Kathy Branze... ...it for anyone who wants to have a ninety-day journey .... ... ..art of God. It is filled with wonderful biblical inspiration and illustrations that give practical help for everyone. However, the true power of this toolkit is the "how to do it" daily for ninety days. Read this great book, faithfully use it, and your life will never be the same!

—Glenn Sheppard, president/CEO of International Prayer Ministries, founding member of America's National Prayer Committee, former senior associate for prayer for The Lausanne Committee for World Evangelism

Kathy Branzell always makes me smile! She is a down-to-earth, real person who lives her faith and shines with the beauty and vitality of Jesus Christ. These ninety morsels of insight in *An Invitation to Prayer* flow out of her own vital experience and are so practical and simple to apply for anyone caught up in the busy grind of life. Slow down and let these brief, no-nonsense daily meditations guide you into deeper intimacy with the One who so lovingly is right now pursuing you to fulfill your unique destiny full of peace, love, wisdom, happiness, and purpose.

—John Robb, chairman, International Prayer Council, www.ipcprayer.org

*An Invitation to Prayer* by Kathy Branzell is going to give you everything you need in practical ways to draw near to God and experience a greater intimacy in prayer. Kathy doesn't just tell you how important that is. She shows you how to draw near.

—Dr. David Butts, president, Harvest Prayer Ministries, and chairman, America's National Prayer Committee

Kathy Branzell is a deeply committed woman of prayer. Her book, *An Invitation to Prayer*, helps us better understand how deeply God loves us as He longs to enable us to live our lives filled with love from him, for him, and for others.

—Paul Cedar, honorary chairman, The Table Coalition

Sometimes prayer is reduced to an activity or a discipline to be checked off each day instead of being about a relationship with a very real Jesus who lives in us, who lives to intercede for us, and who longs to launch us into the deeper waters of love and service for the sake of his kingdom. In *An Invitation to Prayer*, Kathy Branzell will take you on a ninety-day journey to explore intimacy with God through prayer that will forever change how you pray, how you love, and how you serve!

—Kim Butts, Harvest Prayer Ministry

*An Invitation to Prayer* is a book on prayer written by a real life "daily sitting in my prayer closet" author. It is the only book on prayer you need to read. Kathy Branzell has personally taught us the power of prayer by living out her life alongside our ministry. *An Invitation to Prayer* is an excellent resource for all of us who want to experience the reality of the healing, teaching, and redeeming power of prayer with our Pursuer.

—Jim and Martha Brangenberg, radio cohosts,
iWork4Him Ministries, Inc.

# An
# Invitation
# to
# Prayer

*encounter*
**Peace**
*experience*
*gain* **LOVE**
**Wisdom**
*discover*
**Happiness**
*find*
**PURPOSE**

## Kathy Branzell
### foreword by Ronnie Floyd

**BroadStreet**
P U B L I S H I N G

BroadStreet Publishing® Group, LLC
Savage, Minnesota, USA
BroadStreetPublishing.com

# AN INVITATION TO PRAYER:
## DEVELOPING A LIFESTYLE OF INTIMACY WITH GOD

Stock or custom editions of BroadStreet Publishing titles may be purchased in
bulk for educational, business, ministry, fundraising, or sales promotional use. For
information, please email info@broadstreetpublishing.com.

Cover and interior by Garborg Design at GarborgDesign.com

Printed in the United States of America
19 20 21 22 23 5 4 3 2 1

# DEDICATION

I am deeply blessed with family and friends who love the Lord and love me. I want to thank my husband, Russ, for his prayers, his enduring love and support, and for the thousands of books he has purchased for me in my desire to learn, love, and serve the Lord. I want to thank my son, Chandler, and daughter, Emily, for inspiring me to keep going and growing in the Lord. To my parents, Dave and Joyce, my deepest gratitude for raising me to love God, his Word, and the church, and for showing me what serving God looks like on a day-to-day basis. Thank you to my friends who prayed me through this book and throughout life. I thank God for all of you and the happiness you bring into my life as we share and show the love of Jesus together. I love you all!

# Contents

# FOREWORD

I serve as senior pastor of Cross Church and president of the National Day of Prayer Task Force. We are committed to mobilizing unified public prayer for America.

One of the great joys of serving in this role is meeting so many great people. One star that shines so brightly for Jesus Christ is Kathy Branzell. Her unwavering commitment to Christ is one of the many reasons Kathy serves on the board of directors for the National Day of Prayer.

Let me introduce you to Kathy. I've seen Kathy share her heart in vision meetings with our board. Kathy is a prayer warrior and seasoned veteran in prayer. I've seen her support and encourage her husband, Russ, and together live out this vision of prayer. This extraordinary couple is committed to living and leading others to passionately pursue God in prayer.

If you are searching for greater peace, deeper love, godly wisdom, real happiness, or personal purpose in your life, then you have opened the right book. While you may be in search of one or all of these, it is the God of heaven who is pursuing you personally and passionately. At every turn you take in your life, God is there, always inviting you to pray and to talk to him personally.

I believe the Lord is inviting you to walk with him on this ninety-day journey. When you do, your life will never be the same again.

Dr. Ronnie Floyd, senior pastor, Cross Church;
president, National Day of Prayer;
former president, Southern Baptist Convention

# Stop the Chase— Be Embraced

God is pursuing you with all you need and with all he created you to desire. This ninety-day journey will change you by challenging and equipping you, in prayer and God's Word, to stop the chase to be embraced by all you have been searching for—and more.

Everywhere I have traveled, served, and taught, I find that people are looking for these five things—love, peace, wisdom, happiness, and purpose. It does not matter if they are incredibly rich or unimaginably poor, American or another nationality, Christian or not, or what their skin color or cultural background, they are searching for these same five things. They seek to satisfy their need for these in people, purchases, power, positions of authority, and pain-reducing habits that all end in feeling more pain. They exhaust themselves chasing false fulfillment. Meanwhile, God is lovingly inviting us to prayer: a place of relationship, receiving, and rest. God, the divine designer of our hearts and the author of our destiny, knows exactly what we need to be fulfilled and to fulfill his plans. He pursues us, desiring to draw us close and into his presence and provision.

Our core conscience is constantly asking, *Am I safe?* The response is better known as *fight or flight*. If the answer is, *Yes, you are safe*, the second question we seek is, *Am I loved or cared for?* Only when the answer is yes to both of these does the brain ask itself, *What can I learn?* A person who does not feel safe and loved does not have the capacity to learn. Think about that for a moment—think about all the people who go to work, school, and live in relationships who do not have a safe or loving environment either at home, work, or school, but we expect them to focus, learn, and produce every day, not realizing that they are not physically or mentally able to do so. Often, we try to share or listen and learn about Jesus but do not have the capacity to hear and take heart in what is being shared because of these unmet needs.

Each week has a theme that runs throughout all seven days' devotionals. We begin on Sunday, looking at how that theme is found and focused in God and Scripture. The remainder of each week takes the theme to discuss how each of the five needs are fulfilled by God, looking at peace on Monday, love on Tuesday, wisdom on Wednesday, happiness on Thursday, and purpose on Friday. On Saturday we *selah*, pause and ponder how we will believe and behave differently based on what we have learned that week. Saturday will prompt you to review and respond to that week's invitation to prayer and how God embraces you with what you have been searching for in these areas. Each week will challenge and change you as your faith grows in God's embrace.

Through prayer, Scripture, and science, this book will help you realize that in Christ, we are safe, which gives us peace, and we are deeply loved. These allow us to receive the wisdom we need to release wrong thinking and habits and replace them with Spirit-filled attitudes and actions. These enable us to choose happiness, which lifts us to and through purposeful lives.

## DAY 1

# SUNDAY: FOCUSED AND FOUND IN GOD

*In the beginning God created the heavens and the earth.*

GENESIS 1:1 NLT

We begin this ninety-day journey together with the understanding that God created us in his image, with great love and purpose. You are wonderfully made for a wonder-filled life. He pursues you, as Psalm 23:6 says: "Surely your goodness and unfailing love will pursue me all the days of my life, and I will live in the house of the LORD forever" (NLT).

God designed you and all that exists. He has prepared and provided all that you need, and patiently pursues you with his provision in an invitation to prayer. His love for you runs deeper than you can imagine. It is on this path that we will walk together for the next ninety days in Scripture and prayer, to understand how God defines and designed us, and all that we are searching for to live a fruitful, purposeful life.

Every human being searches for peace, love, wisdom, happiness, and purpose. God designed you to want them, and to walk in them with him. You cannot have any of these apart from him. You may have a taste of them, a shallow counterfeit that the world offers, but don't be fooled; if you want the real thing, it can only come from God. You can chase power, positions, possessions, and people to try to fulfill you, but that is not how God designed you, so they will never fulfill that yearning inside of you. For the next ninety days, you are invited to stop the chase to be embraced by all that you have been searching for. To see things from God's point of view and his view of you as he pursues you in an everlasting story that begins before time existed and lasts for all eternity.

## INVITATION TO PRAYER

Heavenly Father, my creator and Lord, thank you for this journey of seeing how you defined and designed me for your peace, love, wisdom, happiness, and purpose. This story is not a fairy tale, not *once upon a time*, but for all time, a true story of the Prince of Peace pursuing those he loves with more than we could ever dream or imagine. Keep me on this journey, faithful to read and reflect every day, as I accept your invitation to pray and wait in your embrace, in your strength, design, and time.

# DAY 2

# MONDAY: PEACE

*For a child will be born to us, a son will be given to us;
and the government will rest on His shoulders;
and His name will be called Wonderful Counselor,
Mighty God, Eternal Father, Prince of Peace.*

ISAIAH 9:6

*Therefore, since we have been justified through faith,
we have peace with God through our Lord Jesus Christ.*

ROMANS 5:1 NIV

Biblical peace is so much more than a sunset on a quiet beach
or reading a book on a balcony with a mountain view. Tranquil
moments are good for the soul, but they are not the sustaining peace we read about in Scripture. Biblical peace is safety
and security found in Christ, the Prince of Peace, who invites
us to peace through salvation. To see how peace is defined
and designed by God, you have two verses today to help you
understand that peace with God can only come from Jesus,
and the peace of God is both earthly and eternal.

Peace can mean a lack of conflict with man, or more importantly, the soul's assured agreement with God—the peace provided by Jesus on the cross. Peace is the calm in the storm as well as the contentment and courage in daily life when one trusts God. Peace is an observable characteristic of faith; as we will study later, it passes understanding and gives Christ followers an opportunity to explain their peace in times of peril.

Peace with God allows us to have those tranquil moments; it allows our minds and hearts to be settled and still. Peace is exhibited in a quiet mind, able to rest instead of churning in constant chaos of responsibilities or the world raging around us. Peace fights the good fight without compromising biblical character or values; it does not run away and cower but seeks resolution found in truth and love. Peace prevails even when circumstances seem to say otherwise, knowing that God is at work in all things for his glory and our good when we love him and desire his purposes to prosper in our lives.

## INVITATION TO PRAYER

Lord Jesus, you are the Prince of Peace and the provider of peace. Thank you for your love that paid my sin debt and brought peace with the Father. Let peace, not panic, prevail and flow from my heart to my words and deeds.

# DAY 3

# TUESDAY: LOVE

*Love is patient and kind; love does not envy or boast;
it is not arrogant or rude. It does not insist on its own way;
it is not irritable or resentful; it does not rejoice at wrongdoing,
but rejoices with the truth. Love bears all things,
believes all things, hopes all things, endures all things.*

1 CORINTHIANS 13:4–7 ESV

*Love* is a complicated word to discuss; it conjures up thoughts and expressions that we have experienced—a dream come true and disappointments. We may picture a precious old couple who have been married for over sixty years, or a string of broken relationships we or someone close to us has stumbled over or even through. Love bubbles up a spring, or sometimes a geyser, of emotions. Most, if not all, of these thoughts and feelings are based on earthly relationships—romantic, family, friend, team or work related, and even people who attend school or church with us.

Love is not supposed to be defined by these experiences; it is defined by God, the one who designed it. To put it in a meme you could post: Love properly defined has a divine design.

14

If you are a parent or even have a beloved pet, you can understand to some extent that training, discipline, and boundaries are all a part of love. So why do we tend to think that God only loves us when we are doing, and getting, everything we desire? Is that what a successful, respectful, and loving relationship looks like between two people? Of course not! Then why would we believe that this is how we experience love from God who *is* love? God designed prayer to be the place where you can know and grow in his love—true love that is always and forever.

Throughout this book, when you read, think, and pray about love, always connect it with God's love that he designed for you to experience and express.

## INVITATION TO PRAYER

Lord, 1 John 4:8 reminds us that "God is love." Real love begins and ends with you, it flows from you, and it is part of your unchanging character from which you created us and gave your Son for us. Your love blesses, disciples, and disciplines us. You authored our days with love and pursue us with love every day. You love us with an everlasting love. Help me to receive and reflect your love.

# DAY 4

# WEDNESDAY: WISDOM

*For the LORD gives wisdom;*
*from his mouth come knowledge and understanding.*

PROVERBS 2:6 ESV

Wisdom is much more than knowledge you get from reading a book, and it goes deeper than understanding that comes through experience and application. Wisdom is received and reflected in your walk with God. Wisdom comes from God. It goes beyond knowing what to say and what to do; it is the character with which to follow through.

Wisdom is aptitude in action that binds together mind, heart, soul, and strength as one walks with God; it is not given in an instant, but over a lifetime through a lifestyle of intimacy with God. Wisdom is learned in prayer as you listen to God, wait on him, read his Word, worship, work, make decisions, and build relationships. Wisdom wraps itself around our everyday routines and weaves itself into discernment and decisions. It first springs from the "fear of the Lord," an awe-filled respect and reverence of God, and then flows from the constant contact we keep in relationship with him.

The book of Proverbs is filled with examples that compare and contrast the lifestyle of a person who is wise with that of a fool. God does not design or desire that any person be a fool. He has designed us with glorifying, kingdom-significant purpose and then equips us for that purpose with all that we need to succeed. Wisdom for every moment of our lives flows through us when we pray and abide in him.

## INVITATION TO PRAYER

Lord Jesus, thank you for your wisdom that is defined in your character and designed for our calling. I want to walk with you, listening for your instructions and inspiration so that I say and do exactly what you destined me to do for your glory and kingdom's gain. I will seek your face and search your Word for wisdom in all things. I do not want to be a fool, and I do not want to make decisions based on emotions, fear, or pressure but by your will. I want you to be at the center of my relationships so that your focus and fruit abound in me and through me. I know that I can only accomplish your will through your wisdom, and I seek it in the stillness of this moment and as I move through each day.

# DAY 5

# THURSDAY: HAPPINESS

*A merry heart does good, like medicine,*
*but a broken spirit dries the bones.*

PROVERBS 17:22 NKJV

Happiness is not a mood; it is a meaning-filled mindset based on the way God defined and designed you. Over two decades of scientific research on happiness now fills bookshelves and medical journals, sharing the science of what Scripture has always said: we are biologically created for happiness. Happiness produces success, not the other way around; it enables us to be "more motivated, efficient, resilient, creative and productive."[1] Neuroscience is a great interest of mine because I love how you hear God whisper, "I told you so," as you read how wonderfully we are created. As you read today's verse, you should note that a happy heart helps bring strength as well as success; there are also numerous medical studies that show how stress and sadness dries up and weakens your bones.

As I reference science throughout this book, please remember that God chooses to reveal himself in many ways, but we must always keep our heart and mind set on the Creator and remember his infinite mightiness will always have some mystery to our finite minds. Science simply studies with earthly education what our heavenly Father created.

*Happy*, as we will see throughout this book, is the word we read as *blessed* many times in the New Testament. What could possibly make you happier than to be created, loved, equipped, and guarded by God? The Bible is filled with messages that bring meaningful and sustaining happiness to our lives and enable us to be successful in our relationships and responsibilities. Like everything else, it is a choice; we can decide what we focus on and if we are going to trash or treasure that thought, emotion, and response.

Real happiness finds its roots in God's love and provision for our lives. Stop chasing success and be embraced by happiness, the emotion that God ordained for your mind and body to run at its optimal level and be successful.

## INVITATION TO PRAYER

Gracious Lord, I will choose to be happy because I recognize that I am blessed. I will focus on your love that provides for my life, and let happiness do its work in my body and brain as you designed it. I will remember your goodness and count my blessings in times of stress or sorrow, knowing my happiness is found in you and not my circumstances. Thank you for designing happiness to strengthen my body, brain, and bones.

# DAY 6

# FRIDAY: PURPOSE

*"And you shall love the LORD your God with all your heart,
and with all your soul, and with all your mind,
and with all your strength." The second is this,
"You shall love your neighbor as yourself."
There is no other commandment greater than these.*

MARK 12:30–31

Let me begin by assuring you that I am not yelling at you because these verses are in all capital letters; it is written in the Bible like this when quoted from other Scripture. However, we could, and possibly should, consider this to be a highly emphasized message. Sometimes we make pleasing God more complicated than it really is. We turn it into a list of dos and don'ts with the idea that we are only *on mission* when we are on a mission trip or participating in church activities. We turn the purpose of having a loving relationship *with* God into an impossible list of responsibilities *for* God.

You were designed by love and for love. God made his purpose for us simple and strategic—love him and love everyone because, like you, they are made in his image with a kingdom purpose. Since the creation of Adam and Eve, God's desire is to be our first love as we live fruitful lives for his glory. Then he gave us his Spirit to enable us to bear his fruit. The focus here is not a list but loving him with *all* our heart (affection), soul (identity), mind (thoughts), and strength (actions). God does not want part of you, he wants all of you. Then he takes the love you give him and produces fruitfulness in *all* the areas of your life.

A life that achieves God's purposes is paved with all of our love for him and accomplished through all of his love for us. Share your love for him in prayer.

## INVITATION TO PRAYER

Heavenly Father, thank you for your love. Your love formed me and enables me to perform all that you purposed for me to accomplish for your great name. Let love be my first emotion, close my heart and thoughts to judgment and hate, and fill me with your thoughts and affection. Prompt me to give you any part of me I have held back; I want to give you *all* my heart, soul, mind, and strength, and love others through your love. Draw me deeper into your love as I pray.

# DAY 7

# SATURDAY:SELAH ...PAUSE AND PONDER

## REVIEW

As you take time to pause and ponder all that you have read this week, set aside a few minutes to reread the verses from the previous six days. As you meditate on these verses, choose one to write down and memorize; let it become the truth that replaces the wrong thinking that you have thrown in the trash. Every time you catch yourself believing and repeating the lie, stop immediately and be embraced with truth by reading or reciting this passage.

## RECORD

Write down in your journal or notebook at least one specific lesson you learned this week that touched your heart and began to transform your thinking. Commit to making it a habit to review and include it in your prayer time. Be still and allow God to embrace you with the desires of your heart.

Praise him in his attributes that strengthen your faith, and thank him for the hope and help that can only come from knowing him in clearer and nearer ways this week.

# Respond

Make a one- to two-sentence plan of how you will apply this lesson in your life—at home, at work, and in the ways you think about yourself and others. Allow the Holy Spirit to prompt you and provide the courage, humility, love, and anything else you might need to embrace righteous thinking and Christlike character.

# Invitation to Prayer

Wonderful Lord, creator of heaven and earth, my creator, I give you thanks and praise. I desire to see people, situations, and myself through your eyes and heart. You define and design peace, love, wisdom, happiness, purpose, and all that exists. You designed every person and every moment for your great purpose and glory. Help me to be embraced by all that you have pursued me with throughout my life. Forgive me when I run from you, when I search for satisfaction and definition in the things and ways of this world instead of seeking you. Help me to redirect my thoughts to you, to detox my mind of the lies I have believed that steal life. Let me be embraced by your truth that strengthens and sustains my life. It is in belonging to you that I have all that I need to accomplish and experience all that you have designed for my days. Thank you!

# DAY 8

# SUNDAY: FOCUSED AND FOUND IN GOD

*In this manner, therefore, pray:*
*Our Father in heaven,*
*Hallowed be Your name.*
*Your kingdom come.*
*Your will be done*
*On earth as it is in heaven.*
*Give us this day our daily bread.*
*And forgive us our debts,*
*As we forgive our debtors.*
*And do not lead us into temptation,*
*But deliver us from the evil one.*
*For Yours is the kingdom and the power and the glory forever.*
*Amen.*

MATTHEW 6:9–13 NKJV

Do you have life all figured out? I sure don't—there is so much I don't know or understand. Do you find yourself spending extensive time or energy trying to discern or define moments or mountains in your life? What are your questions? Do you ask yourself, *Why? What did I do to deserve this?* Do you analyze your emotions, stuff them, or explode? Do you feel alone, left to figure out and fix everything on your own?

God invites you to join him in the throne room of heaven in prayer. He is waiting there, wanting you to turn your habit to define moments into divine moments. He wants you to lift up your cares and let them go into his hands, not playing tug-of-war with your troubles, but casting them because he cares for you. He invites you to stop chasing through the world and come to him to be embraced by all you are looking for.

This week we will explore parts of prayer and when Jesus taught his disciples to pray. Prayer is a respectful, relational conversation with God. He is, above all, holy and supreme. We seek his will, his ways, and his means to meet our needs. We humbly ask his forgiveness of sin and commit to forgive others. We ask for his protection from our flesh and the enemy, as we trust, thank, and praise God with awe.

As we look at each part, add them to your prayer time. Use them when you find yourself distracted by thoughts, feelings, and problems you cannot define. Set your focus on God.

## INVITATION TO PRAYER

Wonderful Lord, thank you for inviting me to pray. I find faith in praising you. I want to thank you for all you have done, and look to you for protection and provision. There is no one and nothing like you. You are the Lord, my Lord, and I love you.

# DAY 9

# MONDAY: PEACE

*Answer me when I call, O God of my righteousness!*
*You have given me relief when I was in distress.*
*Be gracious to me and hear my prayer!*
*But know that the LORD has set apart the godly for himself;*
*the LORD hears when I call to him.*
*Be angry, and do not sin;*
*ponder in your own hearts on your beds, and be silent...*
*Offer right sacrifices,*
*and put your trust in the LORD.*
*There are many who say, "Who will show us some good?*
*Lift up the light of your face upon us, O LORD!"*
*You have put more joy in my heart*
*than they have when their grain and wine abound.*
*In peace I will both lie down and sleep;*
*for you alone, O LORD, make me dwell in safety.*

PSALM 4:1, 3–8 ESV

Today's Scripture is longer than usual, but there is no better teacher. Today's psalm is a beautiful sketch of the peace that is brought out through prayer. The prayer begins with humility, then desperation coupled with praise, followed by a passionate request for help. God promises to hear us when we pray. In this state of distress, the psalmist, presumably King David, wisely lifts his situation to God and professes his trust in God.

He walks out peace, being determined to not sin in the emotion he is experiencing, to search his own heart and keep it pure, and to continue behaving in a way that brings honor and glory as a servant of God. Peace comes through prayer—knowing God hears and helps, our hope grows as we trust him. Peace expands from comfort to joy as David reflects on God's faithfulness and love. This joy fills the soul and strengthens us, and we no longer stew in pain. Finally, like David, we can lie down in peace and sleep because we dwell in the safety of God.

## INVITATION TO PRAYER

Lord, thank you for instructing and inviting us to experience peace as we pray. We cry out to you and listen as you work and walk through the pressures of life with us. We draw close to you and you turn our terror into trust. You give us peace and show your love, through us, to a world that needs your peace and love. There is peace when I cry out, not act out. As I pray, your presence is my joy and peace.

# DAY 10

# TUESDAY: LOVE

*But I will sing of your strength;*
*I will sing aloud of your steadfast love in the morning.*
*For you have been to me a fortress*
*and a refuge in the day of my distress.*

PSALM 59:16 ESV

Praise is the part of prayer that recognizes and rejoices in God's attributes. You often hear two parts of prayer—praise and thanksgiving—spoken together, but it is important to know that they are different. We praise God for who he is, for the qualities and characteristics that make him God. Thanksgiving gives him appreciation for what he does, praise for who he is. Pause for a moment and think or write down all the characteristics of God you can think of, then praise him.

It is important to think about the fact that God loves you because of who you are, not because of what you do. Somehow, we need to be reminded of this over and over again. If you grew up going to church, you were taught the song "Jesus Loves Me." Most children sing this with great joy and volume, as the ending line references where others can find and learn this truth: "Yes, Jesus loves me, the Bible tells me so!" As you read your Bible, highlight God's attributes in one color and his love for you in another color. You are his child, his workmanship, his beloved. Jesus' love says, *I love you so much, I took the punishment for your sin so we can spend eternity together.* Don't let the world and insecurity chip away at the truth of his steadfast, unending love for you. Love him back with joyful praise, and I encourage you to add a song to your prayers.

## INVITATION TO PRAYER

Almighty God, my creator and redeemer, I love you. You know and see everything. You are everywhere and always with me. You are the Alpha and Omega, the beginning and the end, King of Kings, the one true God. Everything has its existence in you; you knit us together and hold us together. You set the sun, moon, and stars in the sky, and at my decision to follow you, you set your Spirit in me. Your perfect love casts out fear, and I walk in faith and courage as I abide in you. Thank you for loving me. I love you!

# DAY 11

# WEDNESDAY: WISDOM

*If any of you lacks wisdom, let him ask God, who gives generously to all without reproach, and it will be given him.*

JAMES 1:5 ESV

The aspect of prayer that people are most familiar with is *asking*. Some of the first prayers people utter are asking for help, answers, a need to be met, a dream to come true, healing from an illness—the list goes on and on. God tells us to ask when we need wisdom to make a decision or discernment for what we are unsure of. He will guide us through unfamiliar territory and rough waters. His wisdom shines light in dark places and exposes people or plans that can harm or help us.

Praise turns our attention on the God who reigns with power and love. It recognizes that he is God and we are not, and responds in worship of him and his supremacy. Crying out trades our distress for peace. Prayer is not just sitting down with a laundry list of "God, please do this" and "give me that." Prayer is a humble, relational conversation asking the God who knows everything, even the intentions of our heart, and sees everything, from the end to the beginning, to intervene in our lives and enlighten our minds with his wisdom that far exceeds anything we could ever muster up on our own.

God does not want you to go it alone, and you are not bothering him when you ask for his help. He is not disappointed in you. How does it make you feel when someone asks you for counsel? How do you treat someone who recognizes your wisdom or expertise, and humbles themselves to ask? You are more than willing to share what you know, to help them, and it usually grows your relationship in the process. Think how much more your loving heavenly Father is pleased when you ask him to speak into the life he gave you. Give him that opportunity now as you pray.

## INVITATION TO PRAYER

Lord, thank you for loving me and leading me. Thank you for your patience and peace. Thank you that I can come and ask you for help and wisdom. You gave me life and purpose, and I desire to delight you with my love, respect, and service. I do not just want to do good, I want to do your will. I need your wisdom and am grateful you give it generously.

# DAY 12

# THURSDAY: HAPPINESS

*Enter into His gates with thanksgiving,*
*And into His courts with praise.*
*Be thankful to Him, and bless His name.*
*For the LORD is good;*
*His mercy is everlasting,*
*And His truth endures to all generations.*

PSALM 100:4–5 NKJV

In prayer, we must remember that we are having a *relational* conversation with Holy God. Yes, he loves us deeply and desires for us to talk with him, but stop and consider how you like to be approached. How do you feel when someone bursts into your room or office complaining, or if the only time someone comes to talk with you is when they need something? A desperate heart can cry out to God for urgent help, but a humble heart does not enter the heavenly throne room with grumbling and complaining.

Pride and bitterness keep company with darkness. The enemy loves a good pity party; it makes you vulnerable to slide right into the pit. God designed us so that thankfulness not only pulls us from the pit but surges helpful reactions throughout our bodies to help us thrive. A grateful heart shines brightly for the God who loves in immeasurable ways but likes to hear us try to count our blessings.

The number of Bible passages, books, and scientific research papers connecting happiness to gratefulness stacks sky high. We know that happiness pours down when prayers are lifted up. In whatever posture you choose—arms raised, knees bent, voices raised, faces lifted or bowed—as we lift our prayers, our heart and emotions are lifted as well. This is not a "glass half full" motivation, but a "my cup runs over" realization that sends messages all over our bodies to rejoice and be happy. Pause now and think of a happy memory to see what happens. Give God thanks for that memory.

## INVITATION TO PRAYER

Gracious God, thank you for your everlasting mercy, enduring truth, and unending love. Lord, you are my hope and salvation. You are my happiness. You are God and I am yours. I choose to meditate on your greatness, count my blessings, and be thankful to you. Please forgive me for complaining. I know that my bad moods and grumbling are not the overflow of a heart filled with love and faith in you, but are satan's foothold in my flesh. I will watch and focus on your goodness; I will enter and abide in your presence with praise and thanksgiving.

# DAY 13

# FRIDAY: PURPOSE

*"And will not God bring about justice for his chosen ones, who cry out to him day and night? Will he keep putting them off? I tell you, he will see that they get justice, and quickly. However, when the Son of Man comes, will he find faith on the earth?"*

LUKE 18:7–8 NIV

In the parable that Jesus tells in Luke 18:1–8, verse one tells us that Jesus is telling this story to teach his disciples to pray and not give up. Do not be deceived by people who tell you to ask once in prayer and then never bring it up to God again. Scripture is clear that we should ask and keep on asking in humility and trust that God will answer and complete his purposes. God desires justice more than we do, but he will not erase free will. He will, however, work "all things together for good for the ones who love God, for those who are called according to his purpose" (Romans 8:28 CEB).

Prayer opens our hearts to hear from God, to gain wisdom and direction. Prayer humbles and lifts us at the same time, to put us in a posture to see from God's point of view and to point us in the right direction. We are opened to be changed and used by God when we pray, and often God will prompt us to participate in the answer to our own prayers.

For example, you may be praying for God to care for a neighbor going through a difficult situation, and God will give you many ideas of how you can help them as he works to care for them as well. You may pray for the restoration of a relationship and be convicted to make the first move and apologize and ask forgiveness. Even if you did not start the conflict, God may call on you to end it.

## INVITATION TO PRAYER

Lord, in the silent moments of my prayers, where I sit and listen for you to bring wisdom, comfort, instruction, or inspiration, I keep my mind clear and can confidently ask, "Is this thought from you, Lord, or me?" I know you will never instruct me to do anything that opposes your Word or character. Please speak clearly and use me for your purposes that your kingdom come and will be done.

# DAY 14

# SATURDAY: SELAH ... PAUSE AND PONDER

## REVIEW

As you take time to pause and ponder all that you have read this week, set aside a few minutes to reread the verses from the previous six days. As you meditate on these verses, choose one to write down and memorize; let it become the truth that replaces the wrong thinking that you have thrown in the trash. Every time you catch yourself believing and repeating the lie stop immediately and be embraced with truth by reading or reciting this passage.

## RECORD

Write down in your journal or notebook at least one specific lesson you learned this week that touched your heart and began to transform your thinking. Commit to making it a habit to review and include it in your prayer time. Be still and allow God to embrace you with the desires of your heart.

Praise him in his attributes that strengthen your faith, and thank him for the hope and help that can only come from knowing him in clearer and nearer ways this week.

## Respond

This week's lessons give you the tools and opportunity to have an extended prayer time today. Feel free to pause and ponder each prompt and sit still and listen for God's response before moving on. Take some moments throughout today to pray about a thought—something you see, hear, or feel. Cover your day in conversation with God, looking for his hand in your life, the beauty in his creation, and the answer to your prayers.

## Invitation to Prayer

Praise him, name his attributes, and lift him up as your God. Take your time. Now confess your sin and ask for his forgiveness. Be specific—don't just pray a one-sentence prayer with a blanket request for all your sin, but ponder your sins and name them. Confess and repent, then thank him for forgiveness. Give him thanks. You have many things to be thankful for; enjoy the happiness you feel as you think about them and express your grateful heart. Intercede for others, then ask for yourself. Be transparent. Talk to him with respect, but be real; he already knows everything about you. Prayer is supposed to draw you closer; it is where you seek truth, not hide it. Humble yourself and express your faith by telling him you want his will to be done in your life and on earth as it is in heaven.

# DAY 15

# SUNDAY: FOCUSED AND FOUND IN GOD

*Thus says God the LORD,*
*Who created the heavens and stretched them out,*
*Who spread out the earth and its offspring,*
*Who gives breath to the people on it*
*And spirit to those who walk in it,*
*"I am the LORD, I have called You in righteousness,*
*I will also hold You by the hand and watch over You."*

ISAIAH 42:5–6

Long before you were born, God said, "Let there be light" (Genesis 1:3 NIV), and there was light. He formed the earth and all that exists. God designed and set all the laws of physics in motion. He formed man and woman and set in motion all our systems—respiratory, digestive, circulatory, etc.—and even a pattern of rest and sleep. Every breathtaking view—sunsets, mountains, oceans, waterfalls, flowers—he created and placed vibrant colors and majestic movement and power into them. Pause for a moment and ponder the expanse of his creation; take a few moments to praise him as the creator and thank him for some of your favorite people, places, and things.

In addition to our functions and features, our complex organs, and the way we learn and grow, he gave us his breath and Spirit. He gave each person a soul—an individual identity, the substance of who we are and who we are in him. He knit eternity together and had you in his thoughts and plans for right here, right now in his righteousness. All of history and every day to come is for him and about him, his story, and his glory. He is the King of Kings, the great I Am, and yet here we find another promise of his love and greatness: "I will also hold you by the hand and watch over you." This promise from an unchanging God holds the same intensity for the people who love and follow him now as it did on the day he said, "Let there be …" and at the time thousands of years ago when God inspired the prophet Isaiah to proclaim and pen them. He created *and* cares for you—always!

## Invitation to Prayer

Lord, the thought of the grandeur of your creation and greatness of your love overwhelms me with gratefulness even though it is more than I can comprehend. You are mighty and your supremacy is too awesome for me to understand, yet you are willing to hold my hand. I love you, Lord!

# DAY 16

# Monday: Peace

*Therefore, having been justified by faith, we have peace with God through our Lord Jesus Christ, through whom also we have obtained our introduction by faith into this grace in which we stand; and we exult in hope of the glory of God.*

ʀᴏᴍᴀɴs 5:1–2

Have you ever been in the middle of a conflict where you knew beyond a shadow of a doubt who the guilty person was, only to have them deemed not guilty? Maybe it was a situation with one of your siblings, a coworker, or even a close friend, and despite overwhelming evidence, they were cleared and grace was served instead of justice. That is what Jesus has done for us. We have peace with God—he is not waiting for you to mess up so he can bring wrath and pain to your life. As a Christ follower, our peace is a result of putting our faith in Jesus; his perfect life and sacrifice is what God sees when he looks at us.

God sees our hearts and our intentions; he knows when we make an honest mistake and when our intentions were pure but somehow things went terribly wrong. He also sees our hurt and our weakness, and provides comfort and strength. Finally, he sees our sin through the lens of the blood of his Son, Jesus, and waits for us to apologize and ask for his forgiveness so that he can set us back on the right path. Before you were born, a path paved with peace was provided by Jesus to a place of grace.

Stop the chase of trying to clean up or cover up your own mess and be embraced by the grace and peace that Jesus had already provided before you were born.

## INVITATION TO PRAYER

Lord Jesus, you are my peace and I thank you for the peace you have given me with the Father. Thank you for taking the wrath and punishment of my sin. Help me to remember that I cannot clean up or make up for my mistakes; I am only declared not guilty in the peace and gift of your grace.

# DAY 17

# TUESDAY: LOVE

*For while we were still helpless, at the right time Christ died for the ungodly. For one will hardly die for a righteous man; though perhaps for the good man someone would dare even to die. But God demonstrates His own love toward us, in that while we were yet sinners, Christ died for us.*

ROMANS 5:6–8

The most important thing you could ever know is that God loves you—all of you. He created you, and you are his workmanship. More than a masterpiece, you are his child. That is a powerful and perfect love! There is nothing you could do to make him love you less or love you more; he does not love you more one day and less the next. Jesus proved that his love is not based on our affection and actions; while we were still sinners, before we were born or knew his name, he knew we would sin and, even so, he died for us. God's love is based on his unchanging character that he *is* love and everything he does flows from his love.

This is not a wishy-washy, fickle, "use you and leave" kind of love. God's love is greater, stronger, and purer than any earthly love you have experienced or even imagined. He will never leave you or forsake you; even his discipline is as much a blessing as any other gift or opportunity, because it flows from his love. Forgiveness flows from his love that desires to have nothing come between you; when you confess and ask for forgiveness, Christ's love, demonstrated on the cross, sweeps away the guilt and shame. His love surrounds you, guides you, and guards you. Stop the chase—let his love flood your heart, your hurts, your responsibilities, and regrets right now—focus on nothing else and be embraced by all the love you have been searching for.

## INVITATION TO PRAYER

Lord, I need your love more than anything else, more than anyone else. Only your love can satisfy my soul and saturate my life. Help me to know your love when I feel lonely or rejected. Let your love lift me when I feel overwhelmed or underappreciated. Thank you for your forgiveness that allows me to freely walk in your love, untangled from sin and shame.

# DAY 18

# WEDNESDAY: WISDOM

*Your hands made me and formed me;*
*give me understanding to learn your commands.*
*May those who fear you rejoice when they see me,*
*for I have put my hope in your word.*

PSALM 119:73–74 NIV

God formed us for his wisdom; made our brains with such magnificent capabilities to learn, perceive, understand and apply knowledge; and created us to walk in close personal relationship with him so that he could turn what we learn into wisdom. Wisdom planned for you before you were born, first to learn his ways and study his Word so that you could know him and make him known. Knowing God is an ever-deepening relationship enabling you to understand many of the ways he disciplines and disciples you. This causes you to be filled with hope and trust that empowers you to be a light in a dark world.

God gave every person the ability to choose. We make choices with every breath we take, millions of them throughout the day. Some choices have become instinct or habit while others cause us to pause and make a decision in the moment. Choosing to trust God is wisdom that the world may mock or misunderstand. Faith is not for the weak minded or uneducated; it is a place in our hearts, a hole in our lives that nothing else can fill or satisfy. God knit us together to need him, to love him, and to follow him. As our creator, he knows us better than we or any scientist ever could. He knows what will bring harm or health, calm or chaos, to us physically, emotionally, mentally, and spiritually. Wisdom chooses to believe the One who knew us before we were born, even though we will not fully understand until we see him in heaven.

# INVITATION TO PRAYER

Father God, before I was born you knew all the wisdom that would be required for the life you desired for me and from me. You knit me together with the ability to learn and to choose—I choose you! I choose to trust you and to grow that faith. I know you have wisdom stored up for me in your Word and in the purposes you have planned. Thank you for supplying all my needs as I seek your wisdom through all of my days.

# DAY 19

# THURSDAY: HAPPINESS

*He has regarded the prayer of the destitute*
*And has not despised their prayer.*
*This will be written for the generation to come,*
*That a people yet to be created may praise the LORD.*

PSALM 102:17–18

Before you were born, God's words and deeds were written down and passed down so that you would know and put your faith in him. When you read the verses before and after these in Psalm 102, they explain that sharing God's deeds, power, faithfulness, and love causes everyone from the powerful to the prisoner to be filled with awe, to pray to him, and to praise him.

Knowing that God responds in his love to your days of praise and problems should bring you unbridled happiness. God loves you, hears your prayers, and guards and guides you on the days that you seem to be receiving all that you desire and in the darkest days when despair seems to surround you. No matter your circumstances, Jesus surrounds and overcomes them with his never-changing, never-ending love. Stop being stressed and be embraced by the happiness of knowing that before you were born, he made sure you had your Bible to read and reassure you.

Who have you told about his faithfulness, how he sustained you with courage or hope that was beyond anything you have ever experienced? Have you shared your stories of unexpected or undeserved favor and blessing that came just at the right moment or met a need or desire you only shared with God in prayer? Tell someone, write it down, post it on your social media, or share a video and tell what Jesus has done so that others, maybe even generations to come, may praise the Lord.

## INVITATION TO PRAYER

Thank you, Lord, for my Bible. Your Word gives me hope and happiness. You prompted men to write each word so that all generations would know you and praise you. In these next moments I will ponder what I have read in your Word and give you thanks and praise for what I have read (do this now). Now I will ponder what you have written on my heart and done in my life, and give you thanks and praise (do this now). Lord, please give me the opportunity today to share these stories with others so that they seek you and give you praise.

# DAY 20

# FRIDAY: PURPOSE

*For we are God's masterpiece. He has created us anew in Christ Jesus, so we can do the good things he planned for us long ago.*

EPHESIANS 2:10 NLT

Does it amaze you that God not only planned for you but had plans *for* you long before you were born? These plans were not just penciled in; they were not just in case. He planned good things, happy, excellent, useful things not just for earth but for his kingdom and glory.

The plans God made for you are strategic and specially designed for you at this time, with these people, in the places you live, work, learn, shop, travel, and worship. He did not make you as a robot or a puppet; you choose to follow or not, obey or not, do good or evil, help or harm. You are precious to God, and he desires for you to take part in his story in these specific days of history.

Stop and take that in for a minute—or more. We spend so much time chasing significance, trying to make a name for ourselves or trying to leave a lasting impact on this planet. Keep in mind that education and employment are tools that God uses to further his kingdom, not ours. When we work hard, and Christlike character is not compromised for titles or money, then we please God and his plans can prosper in us and through us. The reward of delighting God is far more valuable than any earthly riches or recognition.

Success is sweet when it is carried out in God's will and ways. Influence is important when used for good and God. A business, church, city, school district, university, state, and nation thrive when their leaders fear the Lord, but Christ followers are extremely influential in any position, as employee, member, neighbor, student, teacher, or citizen. God's good deeds and his purpose transform lives for eternity. Stop chasing a position and be embraced by the person of influence God created you to be.

## INVITATION TO PRAYER

Thank you, God, for the plans that you have made for me—good plans, important plans for my life and your kingdom. Help me to remember that every day is significant because of your strategic plans for my life. Give me courage and confidence to love people as you have called me and purposed for me to love. Your delight is my reward.

# DAY 21

# SATURDAY: SELAH ... PAUSE AND PONDER

## REVIEW

As you take time to pause and ponder all that you have read this week, set aside a few minutes to reread the verses from the previous six days. As you meditate on these verses, choose one to write down and memorize; let it become the truth that replaces the wrong thinking that you have thrown in the trash. Every time you catch yourself believing and repeating the lie, stop immediately and be embraced with truth by reading or reciting this passage.

## RECORD

Write down in your journal or notebook at least one specific lesson you learned this week that touched your heart and began to transform your thinking. Commit to making it a habit to review and include it in your prayer time. Be still and allow God to embrace you with the desires of your heart.

Praise him in his attributes that strengthen your faith, and thank him for the hope and help that can only come from knowing him in clearer and nearer ways this week.

## RESPOND

Make a one- to two-sentence plan of how you will apply this lesson in your life—at home, at work, and in the ways you think and act toward yourself and others. Allow the Holy Spirit to prompt you and provide the courage, humility, love, and anything else you might need to embrace righteous thinking and Christlike character.

## INVITATION TO PRAYER

My dear Lord and Savior, Jesus Christ, I am overcome with thankfulness that you made a way for me to be forgiven of my sins and have peace with God long before I was born. Thank you for loving me as you knit me together and for your love that holds me together. You created a brain to think and choose, and I choose to love and follow you. I choose your love to be the basis of my happiness, and your purpose to motivate and move me in my actions. I seek you and to do your will. I throw away the thought of being insignificant or an accident, and I received the truth of knowing I am made in your image and am a strategic part of your plan for these days and the lives of others. Open my eyes to the opportunities you have appointed, and may I bless you with every breath and beat of my heart my whole life through.

# DAY 22

# SUNDAY: FOCUSED AND FOUND IN GOD

*Bless the LORD, O my soul,*
*And all that is within me, bless His holy name.*
*Bless the LORD, O my soul,*
*And forget none of His benefits;*
*Who pardons all your iniquities, Who heals all your diseases;*
*Who redeems your life from the pit,*
*Who crowns you with lovingkindness and compassion;*
*Who satisfies your years with good things,*
*So that your youth is renewed like the eagle.*
*The LORD performs righteous deeds*
*And judgments for all who are oppressed.*
*He made known His ways to Moses, His acts to the sons of Israel.*
*The LORD is compassionate and gracious,*
*Slow to anger and abounding in lovingkindness.*
*He will not always strive with us,*
*Nor will He keep His anger forever.*
*He has not dealt with us according to our sins,*
*Nor rewarded us according to our iniquities.*

*For as high as the heavens are above the earth,*
*So great is His lovingkindness toward those who fear Him.*
*As far as the east is from the west,*
*So far has He removed our transgressions from us.*
*Just as a father has compassion on his children,*
*So the LORD has compassion on those who fear Him.*
*For He Himself knows our frame;*
*He is mindful that we are but dust.*

PSALM 103:1–14

All that Jesus offers is beyond anything you could ever think or imagine. This beautiful psalm flows with praise and thanksgiving for all that God is and has done. Let's follow David's example in an extended time of prayer as we prepare to look and love beyond ourselves this week.

## INVITATION TO PRAYER

Lord, I bless you with all my heart, soul, mind, and strength. I bless you for the forgiveness of my sin and as I count my blessings. Thank you for health and healing, for sustaining my life. You have pulled me out of the pit of hell, of darkness and sorrow. Keep me in the light of your love and glory. I bless you as you renew me each day; you are compassionate, patient, and kind. I bless you as you pour these through me to pour out to others. Your lovingkindness is beyond comprehension but not our reach, as you forgive us and go beyond to forget our sin, not holding it against us but sending it from your presence.

# DAY 23

# MONDAY: PEACE

*Now to him who is able to do immeasurably more than all we ask or imagine, according to his power that is at work within us, to him be glory in the church and in Christ Jesus throughout all generations, for ever and ever! Amen.*

EPHESIANS 3:20–21 NIV

This week we will focus on the fact that what we experience from God is beyond anything we could ever think or imagine. We ask according to our experiences and earthly expectations, but God acts according to the riches of his glory. God's peace comes from him, beyond cultural or earthly peace that passes as soon as the phone rings, the baby cries, the door slams.

Experiencing God's peace transcends circumstances because we have placed our circumstances in his care. We have peace because we know that he is our refuge and strength, he cares for us, and he sees the end from the beginning; therefore, we can continue to get up every day and fulfill our responsibilities, knowing that God will take care of the things that are out of our control or abilities.

Once you experience this peace, then you express it. When you are anxious, angry, frustrated, and fearful, it shows all over you—in your facial expression, body language, posture, tone of voice, etc. When you experience God's peace—peace beyond understanding—you must express it with courage, confidence, gentleness, joy, self-control, forgiveness, and more. Peace beyond ourselves equips us to sit in the doctor's office, wait for that promise or promotion, watch for that prodigal to return, fight that addiction, and mourn our losses without imploding our lives. It is overwhelming peace that gives us steady perseverance and calmness of heart when chaos tries to overtake us. No weapon formed against you on earth or by the enemy can take you out of God's arms, so don't let it steal your peace, instead use it as an opportunity to share peace beyond anything anyone has ever seen before.

## INVITATION TO PRAYER

Lord, you are my peace and you give me peace beyond what any earthly riches or relationship could ever provide. Your peace goes beyond today to eternity. Your peace grows in me as I take my eyes off my problems and seek you. Let others see your peace in me and on me, let my words be soft and my walk be strong in you.

# DAY 24

# TUESDAY: LOVE

*That according to the riches of his glory he may grant you to be strengthened with power through his Spirit in your inner being, so that Christ may dwell in your hearts through faith—that you, being rooted and grounded in love, may have strength to comprehend with all the saints what is the breadth and length and height and depth, and to know the love of Christ that surpasses knowledge, that you may be filled with all the fullness of God.*

EPHESIANS 3:16–19 ESV

Christ's love for you goes beyond measure. Just when you think you have experienced it to the outermost fringes of its power, you are swept away to deeper and stronger love that goes beyond imagination. Just when you think you have messed up beyond Christ's forgiveness, he forgives and goes beyond to take away the guilt and shame as well. Just when you think you are too far gone in your harmful thoughts, actions, or addiction, he pulls you out of the pit and walks with you down the road to restoration and then beyond to freedom. Just when you think the marriage is over, you'll lose everything in your debt, or you can't come back from a bad night or year, God spreads his love over you step by step, even carrying you back to solid ground and beyond to victory.

Love beyond teaches us in our trials that would otherwise condemn us to a future of failure. God's love never leaves us and never fails us. It is a love beyond anything we have ever experienced from this world, but it is the love we must express to the world. We need to show love beyond our preference, politics, generation, and color of skin. We need to extend love beyond our hurts, offenses, diseases, mistakes, opinions, and neighborhood. Love goes beyond the wedding day, the labor and delivery room, and the decision to follow Jesus; these are a beginning to more love, stronger love and love beyond us, but they come through Christ in us.

## INVITATION TO PRAYER

Lord, thank you for your love, a love beyond my sin and shame, beyond my dreams but never beyond my reach. Help me to love as you love me. Lead me to love in forgiveness and humility, treating others with the love that I would want to be treated with and beyond.

# DAY 25

# WEDNESDAY: WISDOM

*How blessed is the man who finds wisdom*
*And the man who gains understanding.*
*For her profit is better than the profit of silver*
*And her gain better than fine gold.*
*She is more precious than jewels;*
*And nothing you desire compares with her.*
*Long life is in her right hand;*
*In her left hand are riches and honor.*
*Her ways are pleasant ways*
*And all her paths are peace.*
*She is a tree of life to those who take hold of her,*
*And happy are all who hold her fast.*

PROVERBS 3:13–18

Note how wisdom goes beyond just being smart—it even goes beyond business, school, or making decisions. God's wisdom is connected to peace and happiness, and it allows us to choose what is good and righteous so that our minds and hearts are calm and blessed.

God's wisdom causes us to pause and look beyond the moment to the long-term, even eternal consequences of our decisions. It prompts us to look deeper into the cause of a conflict or the rage in a response, knowing there is a root to every fruit. God's wisdom humbles us when we realize that we don't know what we don't know and allows us to let God see past our own thoughts and vision of the situation. Wisdom beyond us allows grace and mercy to be our guide down an otherwise treacherous path.

God's wisdom surprises us with insight that we know is beyond us. It brings us to decisions that we could have never chosen on our own if left to our own desires or the deceptions of others. His wisdom will shut our mouth when we are about to say something we should not, and open it when we would rather stay out of a situation but he purposes otherwise.

## INVITATION TO PRAYER

Lord, I need your wisdom, the wisdom that goes beyond the surface to your purpose. I need your wisdom that connects with peace, love, happiness, and all that you desire for me. Let your wisdom flow through me to guide and guard me, my mouth, my choices, my actions, and my attitude. I want your wisdom to extend beyond my emotions, beyond my earthly experiences, and into your eternal plans, that I may love and serve you with a wise heart.

# DAY 26

# THURSDAY: HAPPINESS

*Blessed are the poor in spirit, for theirs is the kingdom of heaven.*
*Blessed are those who mourn, for they shall be comforted.*
*Blessed are the gentle, for they shall inherit the earth.*

MATTHEW 5:3–5

I encourage you to read Matthew 5:1–12 sometime today. This section of Scripture is Jesus' teaching known as "the Sermon on the Mount" or "the Beatitudes." Thousands of sermon series and possibly hundreds of books have been written about this section of Scripture because it is rich in meaning and deep in application. For today, let's just look at the fact that Jesus is teaching not only about relief but beyond the resolution to reward.

Jesus is declaring his followers *happy*, because they get to live beyond the hurt, need, or sacrifice. The "they shall be …" is a Christian's reality. Where am I seeing the word *happy*? Forty-nine times in the New Testament, *happy* has been translated from the Hebrew word *makarios* to *blessed*.[2]

Reread these twelve verses and change the word *blessed* to *happy*. Does it sound a little crazy to describe a person who is mourning as happy? Not when you see past the moment with an eternal point of view. We are happy that we had a loved one, for all the memories and moments together. We are happy for relationships, that we have people in our lives and in Christ we will be reunited with them in heaven. Beyond that, we are happy that Jesus is our comfort, and we can count on his promises that console us in our longings and sufferings. This is just a sliver of the meaning of this verse, but we can see beyond the momentary pain to the beyond-our-imagination gain that makes us happy of heart. I cannot imagine the despair that people who don't turn to Jesus suffer. Let him embrace you now.

## INVITATION TO PRAYER

Lord, thank you that I am *happy* in Christ. I know this does not mean that I do not cry, or that I shut out my emotions and act like a robot. It simply means that hurt does not get the last word in my life. Your healing is beyond what the world offers; when I come to the end of myself or my resources, suffer loss, bring unity where there was division, or suffer because I love you, you promise that my *shall be* is beyond anything I can imagine in the moment. That makes me happy!

# DAY 27

# FRIDAY: PURPOSE

*But if we hope for what we do not see, with perseverance we wait eagerly for it. In the same way the Spirit also helps our weakness; for we do not know how to pray as we should, but the Spirit Himself intercedes for us with groanings too deep for words; and He who searches the hearts knows what the mind of the Spirit is, because He intercedes for the saints according to the will of God. And we know that God causes all things to work together for good to those who love God, to those who are called according to His purpose.*

ROMANS 8:25–28

We have become accustomed to instant gratification, so waiting or even having to move through a process tries our patience.

Purpose does not always reveal itself in a day, and sometimes it does not reveal itself at all, but we know that in our weakness God shows up strong. In our pain he weaves goodness and purpose that we might not have designed but that sets us on his path to the destiny he prepared for us. Purpose goes beyond the moment, beyond the day or situation. Purpose changes people as well as situations. It brings possibilities and lessons that carry over into the next season and situation. It touches lives that touch others and spreads beyond what we get to see this side of heaven.

God's purpose for you is lovingly planned and masterfully prepared before it is revealed, a process beyond what we can comprehend. He does not want us to manipulate the timing or the terms, but he does want us to prepare in faith and participate. As God is working all things for his purpose, obey along the way and love beyond and before he reveals his purpose.

## INVITATION TO PRAYER

Lord, I hope for what I cannot see and wait eagerly for you to reveal your goodness and purpose in the days and years of my life. Victory is found by continuing to walk in your ways while waiting and watching for you. In my pain and pleasure, you are God and you are good. Your goodness and love are not situational; they go beyond all earthly measure and understanding, and so I praise you as I prepare and thank you for your good purpose even before it is revealed.

# DAY 28

# SATURDAY: SELAH ... PAUSE AND PONDER

## REVIEW

As you take time to pause and ponder all that you have read this week, set aside a few minutes to reread the verses from the previous six days. As you meditate on these verses, choose one to write down and memorize; let it become the truth that replaces the wrong thinking that you have thrown in the trash. Every time you catch yourself believing and repeating the lie, stop immediately and be embraced with truth by reading or reciting this passage.

## RECORD

Write down in your journal or notebook at least one specific lesson you learned this week that touched your heart and began to transform your thinking. Commit to making it a habit to review and include it in your prayer time. Be still and allow God to embrace you with the desires of your heart.

Praise him in his attributes that strengthen your faith, and thank him for the hope and help that can only come from knowing him in clearer and nearer ways this week.

## Respond

Make a one- to two-sentence plan of how you will apply this lesson in your life—at home, at work, and in the ways you think and act toward God, yourself, and others. Allow the Holy Spirit to prompt you and provide the courage, humility, love, and anything else you might need to embrace righteous thinking and Christlike character.

## Invitation to Prayer

Lord, you are beyond anything I can think or imagine, but I enjoy trying to imagine. My thoughts are on you as I go through my days and as I lie down at night. Our relationship goes beyond my quiet time in the morning, beyond a blessing over my meals, and permeates every moment of my life. You take the words I say and the things I do and give them purpose beyond me and beyond what I can see. You are beyond me yet with me; you are the Alpha and the Omega, who is and who was and who is to come (Revelation 1:8), yet you are with me right now, in this moment, in this breath and heartbeat. I trust you with this day and every day, with the days I don't understand or when I can hardly stand, because you are God and you are good. I love you beyond what my words and life can express.

# DAY 29

# SUNDAY: FOCUSED AND FOUND IN GOD

*"But he who enters by the door is a shepherd of the sheep. To him the doorkeeper opens, and the sheep hear his voice, and he calls his own sheep by name and leads them out. When he puts forth all his own, he goes ahead of them, and the sheep follow him because they know his voice. A stranger they simply will not follow, but will flee from him, because they do not know the voice of strangers." Jesus said to them again, "Truly, truly, I say to you, I am the door of the sheep. All who came before Me are thieves and robbers, but the sheep did not hear them. I am the door; if anyone enters through Me, he will be saved, and will go in and out and find pasture. The thief comes only to steal and kill and destroy; I came that they may have life, and have it abundantly. I am the good shepherd; the good shepherd lays down His life for the sheep."*

JOHN 10:2–5, 7–11

On a recent visit to Israel, I sat and watched two separate herds of sheep on a hill grazing their way closer to one another. Eventually they were all mixed together in one lush spot. One of the shepherds spoke and his herd immediately followed him to another part of the hill, while the other herd did not budge. What a wonderful illustration of knowing and following the shepherd's voice!

Jesus is the Good Shepherd. When you are a Christ follower, you are following the one and only God who cares so deeply that he laid down his life for you. As you spend time studying your Bible, praying, going to church, and knowing him more deeply, you will quickly learn to discern his voice. It is vital to distinguish his voice from the voice of the enemy, who comes to kill, steal, and destroy. Jesus will lead you to peaceful, abundant places where he has made plans for you and will provide for you in stormy and sunny days.

## INVITATION TO PRAYER

Jesus, I want to know your voice, to discern your direction from danger and distraction. Let me hear your voice clearly and know it leads me to places of safety and provision even if I do not see it or understand. I trust in your promises and know you have given me abundant life.

# DAY 30

# MONDAY: PEACE

*This is the message we have heard from him and declare to you:
God is light; in him there is no darkness at all. If we claim to
have fellowship with him and yet walk in the darkness, we lie
and do not live out the truth. But if we walk in the light, as
he is in the light, we have fellowship with one another, and the
blood of Jesus, his Son, purifies us from all sin. If we claim to be
without sin, we deceive ourselves and the truth is not in us. If
we confess our sins, he is faithful and just and will forgive us our
sins and purify us from all unrighteousness.*

1 JOHN 1:5–9 NIV

Love and obedience walks in light without shame. Being tempted is not a sin, but choosing to sin—to disobey God—instead of reaching for him to fight through the temptation, that is walking in darkness. Tragically, research shows that many people who claim to be Christ followers are living in darkness; they have a mindset, a habit, a lifestyle of immorality or an idol that does not reflect the power and fear of God living and working in their life. If we say we follow Jesus and then go to that website, meet or call that person who is not our spouse, go to that clinic, gossip about our coworkers, cheat on our taxes, or spend time throughout the workday surfing, shopping, or playing games on the internet, then we live a lie.

We must confess that we are sinners in need of a Savior. We must admit and take responsibility for our sin, and whole-heartedly ask God for the strength, minute by minute, day by day, to walk away from that sin, resist temptation, and to draw nearer to him. Peace with God starts with knowing we are not perfect but are a work in process that allows God to make progress in us each day.

## INVITATION TO PRAYER

Lord, I need you. I admit that I have sinned. I have (fill in your sin). Please forgive me and cleanse me as only you can. Strengthen me to walk in obedience to you, to be an authentic follower of Jesus. I want to be embraced in your peace and come out of the grip of sin. Please help me to resist temptation and live in the light.

# DAY 31

# TUESDAY: LOVE

*Who is a God like you, pardoning iniquity,*
*overlooking the sin of the few remaining for his inheritance?*
*He doesn't hold on to his anger forever;*
*he delights in faithful love.*
*He will once again have compassion on us;*
*he will tread down our iniquities.*
*You will hurl all our sins into the depths of the sea.*

MICAH 7:18–19 CEB

I am not sure if there is a greater expression of love than forgiveness. Putting another's interest over yours is deeply kind; serving the needs of someone, sharing or even sacrificing what you have for another is tremendous; and all are required in a loving relationship, but forgiveness says *I will choose to go on loving you even though you hurt me deeply*. Forgiveness sets aside self and, in humility, decides to bring love instead of revenge to the situation. Forgiveness does not carry a grudge or keep score, it does not think *they owe me*, or *I'll bring this up next time I goof up*. Forgiveness lets go of the hurt and allows love to heal the wound. Forgiveness leaves the pain in the past, knowing that God has forgiven our own sin and taken away

our shame. Holy God forgives and erases the eternal consequences, and our sins have been cast "to the bottom of the
sea," giving us a picture of depths and darkness so vast they
will never be seen or dug up again.

If you are carrying the guilt and shame of sin, confess
and ask for forgiveness and then *receive* the forgiveness. Let it
wash over you and cleanse you, removing all the shame that
you have been carrying. Love forgives, and living in the love
of Jesus, you can give and receive forgiveness in full. Let that
love embrace you.

## Invitation to Prayer

Lord Jesus, thank you for taking the punishment of my
sin so that I can be forgiven. Thank you for wiping away the
sin and the shame. Help me to walk in the freedom you have
provided. Help me to remember that I am to forgive others
as I have been forgiven—fully and forgotten. I will not forget
the lessons I have learned or the shelter you give me from the
shame. Guide me to your faithful love that heals the wounds of
my sin and makes me whole in your presence. I love you, Lord!

# DAY 32

# WEDNESDAY: WISDOM

*Incline your ear and hear the words of the wise,*
*And apply your heart to my knowledge;*
*For it is a pleasant thing if you keep them within you;*
*Let them all be fixed upon your lips,*
*So that your trust may be in the LORD;*
*I have instructed you today, even you.*

PROVERBS 22:17–19 NKJV

The journey of a Christ follower is mapped out in studying and living God's Word. Answers to tough questions—and tougher emotions—are found in Scripture; knowing what to say or when to keep your mouth shut is learned and discerned throughout the pages of your Bible. Daily Bible study should be as much of a part of the life of a Christ follower as eating and sleeping. It should not be viewed as an optional or recreational activity, although God will give you rest and refreshment as you lay down the burdens and emotions of life and pick up your cross and follow him.

The wisdom of understanding God's story from Adam to you is almost too amazing to comprehend. We are blessed beyond measure to have his story in the pages of the best-selling book of all times. The people, lessons, love, and consequences are written out so that the generations before and after us will know his great deeds and put their hope in him. These stories are not entertainment; they are examples for us to follow, not *once upon a time* but for all times. God's wisdom is for us to trust and tell others, to share with ready answers and prayers. Be embraced by wisdom. Study God's Word every day, not just reading it but meditating on it—think about what you read over and over again. Let it replace toxic or painful thoughts that you churn over and over in your mind, and let it bring peace, love, and wisdom to the relationships and responsibilities in your life. Let Scripture make you wiser and stronger with every passing day.

## INVITATION TO PRAYER

Lord, I love your Word that teaches me truth and to trust you. Your story is a gift to let me see your faithfulness far into the past, and your Word never fails. Your precepts teach me how to abide in you and believe your promises. Show me how to share your love and message of salvation.

# DAY 33

# THURSDAY: HAPPINESS

*Bondservants, be obedient to those who are your masters according to the flesh, with fear and trembling, in sincerity of heart, as to Christ; not with eyeservice, as men-pleasers, but as bondservants of Christ, doing the will of God from the heart, with goodwill doing service, as to the Lord, and not to men.*

EPHESIANS 6:5–7 NKJV

When you become a follower of Jesus you are made new, and as you grow you are given a new view of everything in your life. Understanding that everything you do is for God and not man, that work is worship and learning shows love, should completely change the attitude you have about going to work and school. When you base your emotions on eternal things and let Jesus fill you, there is a love and excitement to see how he will work things out in new opportunities; in all the highs and lows of your circumstances, you can choose to be happy and worshipful because he is a constant, unchanging, and mighty God.

You can choose to be happy because your sins are forgiven and you are free from the guilt and shame that used to weigh you down. You can be happy because God loves you so deeply that he sent his Son to take your sin and defeat death for you. You can be happy and sing a song (aloud or in your mind) of his goodness and blessings, choosing to count them at times when the world tries to drag you down. You can be happy because you read in your Bible today how the weak are made strong, how God always keeps his promises, and how he chose you to be a royal priesthood, his ambassador, his beloved, and his purified priceless possession.

## INVITATION TO PRAYER

Lord, I choose to be your bondservant, to give myself to your will and service. I want all that I do to count for you and your kingdom. I want my attitude, affection, and affirmation to flow from your Word and work in my life. I know that you made me free—removed the shackles of my sin and selfishness—and now I choose to remain in you, happy to be your servant. Let everything I do—my praise and prayers, my studying and obeying your Word, and my worship in song and work—bring you glory. You embrace me with happiness as I keep my eyes on you.

# DAY 34

# FRIDAY: PURPOSE

*Sing to the LORD, bless His name; proclaim the good news of His salvation from day to day. Declare His glory among the nations, His wonders among all peoples. For the LORD is great and greatly to be praised.*

PSALM 96:2–4 NKJV

God created you to have a relationship with him and to share the good news of his salvation every day with the people you encounter. I call this *every day along the way disciple making.* This is the model Jesus gave to us: as he was walking through a city, sitting by a well, on a boat or on a hillside, he prayed, cared for people, and shared the kingdom message with whoever was with him. His words touched the ears of his disciples, the religious elite, the sick, and the sinners who were hurting and helpless and in need of a shepherd (Matthew 9:36).

We should use this same model of praying, caring, and sharing as we go through our days and life. When you became a Christ follower, you also became a disciple maker. No one is excluded from this commissioning—it is not just for pastors and missionaries, it is for every Christian. It does not require you to go around the world, and for some it requires you to simply share across your own kitchen table or across the street. You can share good news across a cup of coffee or lunch, in a casual conversation or a crisis that needs comfort or courage. Jesus is the God of all days and circumstances. Your testimony is not just how you became a Christ follower but how Jesus is present in your life every day. Your testimony is as new each day as breaking news, because he is always guarding, guiding, lifting, teaching, and loving you. Your purpose is to share it with others as he writes his story on through the days of your life. Be embraced by God's greatness and his purpose for you to share good news today.

## INVITATION TO PRAYER

Lord, I want to declare your glory to the nations, but at times I am stumped on how to share it with my neighbor. Thank you for showing me that this is an everyday exercise of talking to friends, family, and others, to share my happiness and hope in your goodness. The culture is distracted by bad news; let my life shine and share your good news.

# DAY 35

# SATURDAY: SELAH ... PAUSE AND PONDER

## REVIEW

As you take time to pause and ponder all that you have read this week, set aside a few minutes to reread the verses from the previous six days. As you meditate on these verses, choose at least one to write down and memorize; let it become the truth that replaces the wrong thinking that you have thrown in the trash. Every time you catch yourself believing and repeating the lie, stop immediately and be embraced with truth by reading or reciting this passage.

## RECORD

Write down in your journal or notebook at least one specific lesson you learned this week that touched your heart and began to transform your thinking. Commit to making it a habit to review and include it in your prayer time. Be still and allow God to embrace you with the desires of your heart.

Praise him in his attributes that strengthen your faith, and thank him for the hope and help that only come from knowing him in clearer and nearer ways this week.

# Respond

Make a one- to two-sentence plan of how you will apply this lesson in your life—at home, at work, and in the ways you think and act toward God, yourself, and others. Allow the Holy Spirit to prompt you and provide the courage, humility, love, and anything else you might need to embrace righteous thinking and Christlike character.

# Invitation to Prayer

My wonderful Savior, thank you for hearing my confession of sin and cleansing me of the guilt through your blood and forgiveness. I will forgive, as you have forgiven me. Thank you for the peace I have with you and in you. Thank you for your love that leads and comforts me, that gives me courage and security beyond that of any human relationship. Thank you for your ever-flowing blessings that are my reasons for happiness and holiness. From my first thought each morning until I lie down to sleep, I want to keep my mind on you and the mission of sharing your love and message with others. Thank you for the wisdom I can study in your Word and your great deeds that I can share every day. As I follow you, help me to grow in peace, love, wisdom, happiness, and purpose. I am your disciple and I will make disciples by sharing your good news and glory.

# DAY 36

# SUNDAY: FOCUSED AND FOUND IN GOD

*Remember the Sabbath day and treat it as holy. Six days you may work and do all your tasks, but the seventh day is a Sabbath to the LORD your God. Do not do any work on it.*

EXODUS 20:8-10 CEB

Why does God command you to rest? Because God created you to rest. God was so serious about this that according to Exodus 31:15, a person who worked on the Sabbath was "to be put to death." Science now shows us that working more than a six-day work week is life-threatening.[3] Research shows in great detail the serious health problems, decreased productivity, and increased depression, addictions, and relationship problems caused by working over forty to fifty hours per week. Increased stress from less rest causes weight gain and problems with sleep, the immune system, memory, and more.

God has desired to protect us from this since he first created man. When God called his people out of slavery in

Egypt, they had been abused slaves, forced to work long hours under harsh overseers. God was readjusting their lives to rest, not to being slothful, but rested to give their best and trust him with all that they needed to do. Our responsibilities are important—a vital part of paying our bills and contributing to our workplace and society. All of these have kingdom value. As followers of Jesus we strive to give our best, but we must also rest.

According to the National Sleep Foundation, getting enough sleep enables better decisions and fewer mistakes, avoids burnout, improves memory, and helps to recover your focus more quickly after being interrupted or distracted.[4] Once again we can hear God whisper, "I have been telling you that for thousands of years." Rest!

# INVITATION TO PRAYER

Lord, thank you for enabling me to work and calling me to rest. Thank you for the rhythms you set in our bodies for them to be productive and refreshed. I do not want to be lazy, nor do I want to work myself to death. I look to you and trust you with all that is on my schedule, all that my job requires of me, and I know that if I obey your command to rest, you will multiply my time and mind to get things done in a way that also brings you all the glory.

# DAY 37

# MONDAY: PEACE

*Casting all your anxiety on Him, because He cares for you.*

1 PETER 5:7

What do you think of when I say the word *rest*? Do you think about taking a nap? Getting eight hours of sleep? Taking a vacation or a long walk? So often we only think about our body and forget that our minds need rest too. The fact is, if we do not rest our thoughts, then the long walks and vacations create more stress, not less, because all we think about is all the work we are not getting done at that moment and the problems that wait for us when we get back.

Rest—real rest—involves giving our cares to Jesus and focusing on how strong he is instead of how heavy our burdens seem. Our faith—real faith—permeates our whole lives; it is not just about who we will worship on Sunday, but who we will trust and worship every day.

Instead of running your burden through your mind over and over again, rest. Cast your cares, your hurts, the decision you need to make, the problem you can't figure out—whatever it is—on Jesus. Give it to him and rest. It might be difficult at first, so commit to giving it to him for an hour while you nap or take a walk. Tell him that you are trusting him with the situation and solution, and then focus on something or someone that brings peace and happiness to your life. Stop the chase filled with anxiety and be embraced by God's rest as you trust him with all the answers.

## INVITATION TO PRAYER

Lord Jesus, I trust you. I am resting in you—choosing to open my mind and life to let your power and supremacy permeate every anxious thought, hurt, doubt, and decision. Help me to rest; help me to hand over every aspect of my life and rest in the security of your arms instead of wrestling with my anxieties. Help me to clear my mind and my calendar to rest and be refreshed in you. Enable me to quiet the noise around me as well as the roar in my mind so that I can enjoy silence. I want to embrace rest and remove stress from the way I process this wonderful life that you have given me.

# DAY 38

# TUESDAY: LOVE

*Come to me, all who labor and are heavy laden, and I will give you rest. Take my yoke upon you, and learn from me, for I am gentle and lowly in heart, and you will find rest for your souls. For my yoke is easy, and my burden is light.*

MATTHEW 11:28–30 ESV

Love calls you to rest. In these verses we can picture Jesus possibly sitting by the Sea of Galilee seeing or recalling a boat they had seen earlier that was "heavy laden," a nautical term for a boat that is carrying more than it was built to carry and is in danger of tipping or sinking. Have you ever felt that way? Do you feel that way right now—that you are carrying more than you can handle? Are you overwhelmed and overburdened, and do you feel yourself sinking under the weight and waves?

Maybe, just maybe, this is where Peter was inspired to write, "Casting all your care upon Him, for He cares for you" (1 Peter 5:7 NKJV). Jesus loves you and did not mean for you to carry all of these burdens on your own. Be still for a moment and let him inventory your cargo—what all are you carrying? (Name some things now that are weighing you down.) Stay still, and catalogue your thoughts, responsibilities, hurts, and worries—oh, there's one—then toss the worry to him and let him replace it with much lighter peace. What are you carrying that is not yours to carry? You cannot *make* people happy. You can love them, but they must choose their mindset or mood. Is unforgiveness in one of those boxes? Time to toss it and allow healing to begin. There—doesn't that feel better already? Bills? Job stuff? Family? Schedules? Conflicts? Maybe even something heavier, like a diagnosis or an eviction notice? Hand them over in prayer to the One who loves you and wants to lighten your load; let him give you rest.

## INVITATION TO PRAYER

Lord Jesus, I come to you now accepting your invitation to rest. I am weary, worried, or just plain worn-out, and I need your love to wash over me and wash my worries overboard. Lift me with your love so that I do not sink. Show me where I have picked up cargo that is not mine to carry, and I will cast it to you.

# DAY 39

# WEDNESDAY: WISDOM

*When a wise man has a controversy with a foolish man,*
*The foolish man either rages or laughs, and there is no rest.*

PROVERBS 29:9

How do you react to controversy? What do you do when someone opposes you, when they take the opposite stance? Do your debates escalate in volume or spread into areas that have nothing to do with the initial subject? Does your conversation quickly slide into sarcastic remarks or rage into a range of emotions you have bottled up? As you read this, were you imagining these reactions coming from other people or coming out of yourself? Pause and think it through; be honest with yourself but don't beat yourself up.

We might define controversy as a conflict between two or more people, but many times it comes from within. How do you talk to yourself? Do you slice yourself with sarcasm, call yourself ugly names, or let your mind race to every mistake you have ever made and drag the past into your present situation? Stop! Give yourself a break by breaking up with the pain of your past and let the wisdom of God rush into your current situation. Stay calm and stay present; rest in God's forgiveness and faithfulness in your past, and let him fill your mind with wisdom in this moment.

We cannot control other people's actions or emotions, but we can choose to control our own. Stop the chase that causes your mind and mouth to race to places that bring more conflict, and let God embrace you with wisdom that allows love and peace to flourish in and around you. Rest in the moment. Don't race back to the past or forward to the finish line; let God guide you at his pace to the place where victory waits for you.

## INVITATION TO PRAYER

Heavenly Father, it is hard for me to imagine victory *waiting* on me. I have always pictured a race being a place of running full steam ahead. Just when I think I have left the past behind, something triggers my anger, regret, or pride, and I realize that I am carrying the past around instead of casting it. I leave my past with you where your love and peace can reshape it into wisdom and I can rest and not rage. Give me the wisdom to see controversy as opportunity, not opposition.

# DAY 40

# THURSDAY: HAPPINESS

*I know that nothing is better for them than to rejoice, and to do good in their lives, and also that every man should eat and drink and enjoy the good of all his labor—it is the gift of God.*

ECCLESIASTES 3:12-13 NKJV

Every moment of your life is a gift from God. Every laugh, smile, tear, trial, lesson, meal, relationship, sunset, and even sleep is from him. Rest is commanded by him; we are to sabbath, to rest and not work seven days a week. By resting we show our trust in him; we obey his boundaries as we protect our time and energy for everything he has planned for our lives.

Rest gives us time to relax and do fun things with others. It builds our relationships with friends and family. It gives us opportunities to meet our neighbors and make new friends. It is a time of recreation or a nap on the couch that refuels us for the upcoming week. Lack of rest leaves us grumpy and unable to focus, and it weakens our immune system and leaves us vulnerable to mood swings instead of all the good that rest brings.

Have you ever been made to feel guilty because you were delighted over a gift, went on a nice trip, or even took the time for yourself each day for prayer and Bible study? Do not feel shallow or misguided if thinking about a vacation or the idea of reading your favorite book in a few minutes of peace and quiet makes you happy. Be embraced with precious moments from God, thank him for them, and trace your smile back to your Savior who wants you to savor the life he has given to you. While vacation is not the purpose of your life, rest and relationship are key components according to Scripture; therefore, you can thank him for special times, in places he created, with people he gave you to love and share life with for his glory. Celebrate rest!

## INVITATION TO PRAYER

Lord, thank you for times of rest—for a good night's sleep, a Sunday afternoon stroll, and times that build my relationships and refresh me to love and serve with strength and kindness. Thank you for wonderful memories from the past and dreams for the future. Thank you for commanding rest and not endless work, and for promising rest to all who come to you.

# DAY 41

# FRIDAY: PURPOSE

*Therefore humble yourselves under the mighty hand of God, that He may exalt you at the proper time, casting all your anxiety on Him, because He cares for you.*

1 PETER 5:6–7

If you had read these verses together at the beginning of this week, it might have felt a little confusing. How can you be elevated by bringing yourself low? What does casting your cares have to do with humility?

Throughout this week we learned that God's hands are a safe and loving place to confess and cast the anxieties that weigh us down and wear us out. This process professes our need for and trust in God. Humility says, *I cannot meet all my needs or fight all my fears on my own.* Humility punctures our pride and deflates our ego so that we see ourselves and God in the correct proportion. God is almighty and all-powerful, and we are not. What's even better is to see how small and light our problems are when they are lifted by God instead of loaded on us.

Casting our cares on him clears our vision and reserves our strength for the plans that God has for us today. Casting empties our minds, hearts, and hands of chatter and clutter so we can see and respond to the opportunities of the day. Casting also catches the attention of other people, who wonder how we keep our cool when we are under fire or smile confidently while uncertain circumstances surround us.

Some crises come so we can learn and grow from the experience, or to give us the opportunity to comfort and serve others. Every situation gives you the opportunity to see new and familiar ways that God cares for you; as you grow, he is glorified. He will lift you up as you lift up prayers of praise and faith.

## Invitation to Prayer

Lord, I humble myself under your mighty hand that lifts, and not crushes, me. Your hand guides and provides for me. Your hand is a shelter that shades and sustains me—the authority I trust and obey. Your strength is all I need to get through each day, in every smile and every trial. Thank you for loving me. I can rest knowing that everything I encounter has to come through your hands first; you prepare me and provide all that I need at just the right time, so I can rise above my circumstances into your embrace.

# DAY 42

# SATURDAY: SELAH ... PAUSE AND PONDER

## REVIEW

As you take time to pause and ponder all that you have read this week, set aside a few minutes to reread the verses from the previous six days. As you meditate on these verses, choose one to write down and memorize; let it become the truth that replaces the wrong thinking that you have thrown in the trash. Every time you catch yourself believing and repeating the lie, stop immediately and be embraced with truth by reading or reciting this passage.

## RECORD

Write down in your journal or notebook at least one specific lesson you learned this week that touched your heart and began to transform your thinking. Commit to making it a habit to review and include it in your prayer time. Be still and allow God to embrace you with the desires of your heart.

Praise him in his attributes that strengthen your faith, and thank him for the hope and help that can only come from knowing him in clearer and nearer ways this week.

## Respond

Make a one- to two-sentence plan of how you will apply this lesson in your life—at home, at work, and in the ways you think and act toward yourself and others. Allow the Holy Spirit to prompt you and provide the courage, humility, love, and anything else you might need to embrace righteous thinking and Christlike character.

## Invitation to Prayer

Thank you, Lord, for calling me to rest and to trust you with everything on my schedule and on my mind. Lord, help me to stop taking on more than I am purposed to do. I do not want to steal other people's blessings or lessons by swooping up jobs you never meant for me to do. Open my eyes, heart, and schedule to the opportunities you designed for me—even when they are out of my comfort zone or zip code—so that your strength and love shines, not mine. Help me to invest my time wisely on the people and places you put in my life. Keep me from feeling guilty when I sit down or even lie down for a few minutes of rest or a sabbath nap. Keep me from running ahead or from lagging behind, and keep me under the embrace of your yoke, walking right beside you.

# DAY 43

# SUNDAY: FOCUSED AND FOUND IN GOD

*And this is the reason: God lives forever and is holy.*
*He is high and lifted up.*
*He says, "I live in a high and holy place,*
*but I also live with people who are sad and humble.*
*I give new life to those who are humble*
*and to those whose hearts are broken."*

ISAIAH 57:15 NCV

God is not some far-off king hidden behind high walls and armed guards to whom you have no access. Nor is God some father figure that you just come to for advice or an allowance. God is high and holy yet is with you and in you. As you abide in him and he in you, you are sheltered in the shadow of his wings and live under and in his authority. His thoughts toward you are too high a number to ever count, and his embrace of you is a seal that the enemy cannot break.

His words are so powerful they created all that exists; he spoke all space, matter, and time into existence. Then, in a love that is higher than we could ever fathom, he sent his one and only Son, who is fully God, to become fully man to pay a price higher than any human could ever pay. Jesus suffered the wrath of God and was raised from the dead so that he could lift us up to the Father. He is not some far-off spirit floating through the clouds, but living in you, guiding, guarding and growing you every day. God is high yet here, beyond yet bringing you along, always and now. God is more than we could ever comprehend, and his love and power never end, but he is closer than any friend.

## INVITATION TO PRAYER

Lord, you are always and forever, over and surrounding, high but you hear my prayer. As I try to ponder you, I am in awe and wonder. My mind cannot grasp how you are high yet here, but my heart believes. Your presence is my comfort and courage, my love and life. Your power is my protection, and you author and advance my purpose as you lift me up to tell me your thoughts and you walk with me to show me your ways. My heart is lifted to do your will, my arms lifted high in worship, my God, most high!

# DAY 44

# MONDAY: PEACE

*For the weapons of our warfare are not of the flesh but have divine power to destroy strongholds. We destroy arguments and every lofty opinion raised against the knowledge of God, and take every thought captive to obey Christ.*

2 CORINTHIANS 10:4–5 ESV

Your brain is an amazing creation and a great example of God's love and desire for a real relationship with you instead of making you a puppet or robot. God gave you the ability to make choices and think through situations and decisions, counting the cost of consequences and outcomes and then choosing for yourself how you will proceed. Free will is a basic ingredient of quantum physics[5] and neuroplasticity—your ability not just to change your mind but to actually change the patterns and processing paths of your brain. The old excuse of *that's just the way I am* or *you can't teach an old dog a new trick* is not scripturally or scientifically valid.

The way that you decide to react to your feelings and the attention you give each thought determines how your brain functions. You have the power to detox hurtful, sinful, and untruthful thoughts and replace them with higher, holy truth that not only changes your habits but your health as well.[6] If you need to repent of something, confess and repent. If you have a need—if you need strength, wisdom, forgiveness, peace, or anything else—pray and ask God for it. Speak truth over your life and see yourself as God sees you, through eyes of love and redeemed in Christ's blood.

## INVITATION TO PRAYER

Lord, I repent for thoughts that keep me awake, what I stew on, and the loops of anger, anxiety, or regret. I do not want my thoughts to steal my peace. I need your strength, and I will meditate on your truth and toss the thoughts that are trash. I know I have a choice; I will take each thought captive and ask myself, *Is this thought from God or is it garbage?* I will replace fear with thoughts of your faithfulness. "In peace I will both lie down and sleep, For You alone, O LORD, make me to dwell in safety" (Psalm 4:8).

# DAY 45

# TUESDAY: LOVE

*Your love, LORD, reaches to the heavens,*
*your faithfulness to the skies.*

PSALM 36:5 NIV

What do you think of when you hear the word *love*? Do you think of an experience like a warm tingly feeling or an expression like flowers and gifts? You may feel pain for love that was lost or false. You may think of a first kiss or your wedding day. Do you connect love with Valentine's Day or every day? Do you think of someone, or a group of people like your family? Do you think of God?

God is love and loves you. Yes, I have said this before, but Scripture says believing comes by hearing and science says it must be repeated to be remembered. Despite any earthly love, great or hurtful, nothing will ever come close to the love of God. It is beyond anything you can ever think or imagine. It is greater than any human can give and is higher than we could ever achieve.

If you have been hurt by love, think higher; God's love comforts and defends. If you have been rejected, think about the great love that gave you life and then gave his life for you.

If you have been abandoned, know that God will never leave you or forsake you. If you have been abused or neglected, cry out to God, whose love nurtures and protects.

This broken, hurt-filled world still waits for the day when Jesus will return and set all things right. Until that day, God's love penetrates our pain and suffering to bring healing and hope. Love uses the enemy's fire to take us higher—to lift us to new heights where we can love deeper and stronger than we ever imagined. Stop chasing a feeling and let God embrace you with his love that will lead you and lift you, to and through love.

## INVITATION TO PRAYER

Lord, as I sit here embraced by your love, I rejoice that you know what is in my heart—the needs, the hurts, the joy in my past, present, and future. You see the beginning from the end, and your love stretches through the ages and through my circumstances to help and hold me. I exist because of your love, and as I seek you I can experience higher love, deeper love, and unending love every day. You are love and I am loved!

# DAY 46

# WEDNESDAY: WISDOM

*For my thoughts are not your thoughts,*
*neither are your ways my ways, declares the LORD.*
*For as the heavens are higher than the earth,*
*so are my ways higher than your ways*
*and my thoughts than your thoughts.*

ISAIAH 55:8–9 ESV

Currently there is a popular saying that encourages, "When others go low, we go high." It inspires us to rise above the bullies, the critics, and the culture that tries to pull us down and calls on us to take the high road throughout life. It is great advice, but God calls us even higher, to go above and beyond what we think to transcend the hurt and hate. The only way up is down—bowed down in prayer that leans in to listen and learn his higher thoughts and ways.

This wisdom comes from his Word; it is a higher education from on high, from the One who calls and conforms us into the character of Christ. This is not a position of putting ourselves down in criticism or shame, but a right view in humility and worship. It is wisdom that is higher than us but not beyond us if we come willing to not ignore but *love* those who seek to put us down. It is more than refusing to participate in the selfishness and sin, but a willingness to overcome with prayer, love, and lifting up Jesus to people who are mean and mad. Higher wisdom does not ask, *Why?* but *Whom?* Whom can I show and share your love to, Lord? We don't just rise above; we take those who are low with us, to higher ground. God says, "Take the high way, my way, and let me lift you up in due time." Stop chasing the fight or fleeing in fright and be embraced by the wisdom that will show you what's right.

## INVITATION TO PRAYER

Lord, I come to you and bow low so you can lift me up to know your thoughts and walk in your ways. I cannot see these through the lens of pride or by my power, but only as I seek your face while I am on my face. You are God and I am not, and your wisdom knows the whole story—the hearts, minds, and lives of those who are hurting themselves and others. Prompt me to pray and not judge; show me how to love in ways that lift them up to see you and your perfect love.

# DAY 47

# THURSDAY: HAPPINESS

*Therefore as you have received Christ Jesus the Lord, so walk in Him, having been firmly rooted and now being built up in Him and established in your faith, just as you were instructed, and overflowing with gratitude.*

COLOSSIANS 2:6–7

"The only way to create a more satisfying, fun, fulfilling, and successful life, is by building incrementally higher levels of trust every day."[7] How can you accomplish this? By turning to God and learning to trust him every day. In Christ you are anchored like a tree with deep roots, and you grow higher, being built up as God reveals his faithfulness to you personally in the stories we read in the Bible and in the testimonies of other Christ followers.

Keeping a journal of prayer requests and how they were answered is an undeniable, quick reference to see how God lifts you to safety or guides you to a "higher education" through experiences you probably would never have chosen but now you would never trade. Some of our most intimate times with God are found in the valleys of life, in the shadow of death or destruction, but his embrace kept the shadow from reaching us, his Word was the light on a dark path, and his love lifted us to heights we never knew we could reach.

Pause for a moment or two and think about a specific prayer request that God answered in an extraordinary way, then overflow with thankfulness. Think of a valley he walked through with you, even carried you through. Now overflow with thankfulness. God's lesson plan is to keep you deeply rooted in him, to build up your faith through lessons of his faithfulness, power, and love. Those lessons grow and guide you with every beat of your grateful heart. Gratefulness is connected to happiness in countless studies. Happiness and gratefulness go hand in hand, and they both come from holding the hand of God throughout life.

## INVITATION TO PRAYER

Lord, thank you for all that you have carried me through—for your faithfulness and even for the tests and trials that you used to strengthen my trust in you. I can walk in gratefulness and happiness because my confidence is in you. I want the thankfulness in my heart to overflow to my lips, to keep me from grumbling and instead give you glory in every circumstance. My hope and happiness are only found in you.

# DAY 48

# FRIDAY: PURPOSE

*Two are better than one because they have a good return for their labor. For if either of them falls, the one will lift up his companion. But woe to the one who falls when there is not another to lift him up. And if one can overpower him who is alone, two can resist him. A cord of three strands is not quickly torn apart.*

ECCLESIASTES 4:9–10, 12

God never called us to go it alone. He created us for relationship with him and with the people he placed in your path. Your relationships have higher purpose. Beyond having someone to go to the movies or to study with, beyond doing life together, our presence has purpose in one another's lives. We learn together, work together, and even fight evil together. One of the greatest relationships that we can have is a prayer partner, someone who prays both for us and with us.

Satisfying relationships not only make us happy, they make us healthy.[8] Happy people are generally motivated and not overwhelmed; as they face new and challenging situations, they choose to use coping patterns and support strategies they have developed in past stressful experiences.[9] Your coping pattern of prayer and support strategies from Scripture and godly relationships take the stress out of the test.

Surround yourself with godly counsel and interact with those who will pray and journey with you. The idea of being a lone ranger is not biblical, and science has proven it not only kills your chances of success but may kill you, as loneliness is as deadly as smoking and alcoholism.[10] Live long lives on purpose with others; your love is a lifesaver.

## INVITATION TO PRAYER

Lord, thank you for lifting me higher and making me stronger in our relationship and through relationships with others. Thank you for creating us to love, and that it is not good for man to be alone, that two are better than one. Thank you for the people in my life. Thank you for my prayer partners, for those who laugh, cry, glorify, and trust you together. Thank you for bringing me into your family by your sacrifice on the cross, and for purposing me to share your love and message to expand the family of God.

# DAY 49

# SATURDAY: SELAH ... PAUSE AND PONDER

## REVIEW

As you take time to pause and ponder all that you have read this week, set aside a few minutes to reread the verses from the previous six days. As you meditate on these verses, choose one to write down and memorize; let it become the truth that replaces the wrong thinking that you have thrown in the trash. Every time you catch yourself believing and repeating the lie, stop immediately and be embraced with truth by reading or reciting this passage.

## RECORD

Write down in your journal or notebook at least one specific lesson you learned this week that touched your heart and began to transform your thinking. Commit to making it a habit to review and include it in your prayer time. Be still and allow God to embrace you with the desires of your heart.

Praise him in his attributes that strengthen your faith, and thank him for the hope and help that can only come from knowing him in clearer and nearer ways this week.

## RESPOND

Make a one- to two-sentence plan of how you will apply this lesson in your life and in the ways you think and act toward God, yourself, and others. Allow the Holy Spirit to prompt you and provide the courage, humility, love, and anything else you might need to embrace righteous thinking and Christlike character.

## INVITATION TO PRAYER

Lord, I lift my eyes and heart to you. You are high and lifted up yet dwell with the contrite and lowly of spirit to revive and refresh us. You lift us up to your vantage point to see your heart and follow your commands. Thank you for lifting me higher so I can know you more. You are God Most High, the one true God in whom I put my trust and give my life. You see the end from the beginning, nothing escapes your attention, and there is nowhere hidden from your sight. When I lift my arms in worship and awe, you embrace me with your love; when I lift up my requests for wisdom, you give generously. When I am being pressed or stressed by this world, you embrace me with peace and happiness. Every moment of my life is yours, for your purposes. May your kingdom come and will be done in my life as it is in heaven.

# DAY 50

# SUNDAY: FOCUSED AND FOUND IN GOD

*I love you, O LORD, my strength.*
*The LORD is my rock and my fortress and my deliverer,*
*my God, my rock, in whom I take refuge,*
*my shield, and the horn of my salvation, my stronghold.*
*I call upon the LORD, who is worthy to be praised,*
*and I am saved from my enemies.*
*The cords of death encompassed me;*
*the torrents of destruction assailed me;*
*the cords of Sheol entangled me;*
*the snares of death confronted me.*
*In my distress I called upon the LORD;*
*to my God I cried for help.*
*From his temple he heard my voice,*
*and my cry to him reached his ears.*

PSALM 18:1–6 ESV

I encourage you to write this verse in a journal and on a Post-it note. Circle or underline all the attributes of God and post it where you will see it, recite it, and memorize it. Let God's attributes replace lies of weakness, because he is your strength. You are not insecure or exposed, because God is your security and the shield that surrounds you. You have been set high in his stronghold, and despite the circumstances that encompass you, the Lord empowers you through the torrents and trials that seek to snare you or trip up your faith. You cannot be defeated. He hears your cry for help that invites him into your situation to shelter and save you. His righteous anger burns against the enemy who seeks to kill, steal, and destroy, and God comes to our rescue and restores us with his love. You are never alone. God is always with you and all you need every day; no matter what you are facing, he will fight for you.

# INVITATION TO PRAYER

Lord, as I read beyond these verses, your psalmist says,

*"They confronted me in the day of my calamity,*
*But the LORD was my stay.*
*He brought me forth also into a broad place;*
*He rescued me, because He delighted in me" (Psalm 18:18–19).*

Thank you for the assurance that you watch over me and war for my safety and salvation. You are my rock and my strength, you are my Lord and my love. I will look to you alone to shield and sustain me as I store your Word and will in my heart. You are my everything.

# DAY 51

# MONDAY: PEACE

*This I recall to my mind,*
*Therefore I have hope.*
*The LORD's lovingkindnesses indeed never cease,*
*For His compassions never fail.*
*They are new every morning;*
*Great is Your faithfulness.*

LAMENTATIONS 3:21-23

Troubles have been a part of life since the first bite of forbidden fruit in the garden of Eden. The good news that strengthens and sustains us is that sin did not stain or change God. He is the unchanging God whose attributes are steadfast and always reliable. Circumstances, time, our behavior, and even satan cannot change God in any way. Therefore, you can be assured that in every tribulation you encounter, you can pass through it with peace, knowing that the Lord's lovingkindness and compassions never cease or fail.

The strategy is to make God your first thought every morning; recite the truth that his lovingkindness and compassion are new for you this day and every day. Then let God be your go-to thought replacing fear, pity, anger, or whatever your usual thought or escape might be. Picture God beside you, protecting you as a fortress around you. Instead of trouble surrounding you, envision his angels standing guard and his Word lighting your path to safety and success. Stop letting your imagination run wild with the old habits of fight or flight, and be embraced by peace as you remember God's faithfulness and all that he has carried you through. Think about the things you feared that did not harm you, or the defeat you feared but blessing and victory prevailed. Stop for a moment or more and concentrate on all the answered prayers and surprise endings that God has embraced you with when you waited for him to act instead of raging or running. Be embraced in his hope and help again.

## INVITATION TO PRAYER

Lord, you are the never-changing God whose love is never-ending. I will seek you with all my heart and trust you with all my days; you are my hope and my reward. I will recall all of your goodness toward me, giving me life, love, and salvation. You not only sustain me but surround me with your protection and provision. I will remember your faithfulness and walk in the peace of the One who never turns his back on me, who never fails me and never will.

# DAY 52

# TUESDAY: LOVE

*Two are better than one,*
*Because they have a good reward for their labor.*
*For if they fall, one will lift up his companion.*
*But woe to him who is alone when he falls,*
*For he has no one to help him up.*
*Again, if two lie down together, they will keep warm;*
*But how can one be warm alone?*
*Though one may be overpowered by another,*
*two can withstand him.*
*And a threefold cord is not quickly broken.*

ECCLESIASTES 4:9–12 NKJV

What if I told you that the key to getting through the trials and tribulations of life is love? Okay, what if science told you what God has been telling us all along? Simply search "stress and the role of social support" and study after study shows that, as the Lord God said, "It is not good that man should be alone" (Genesis 2:18 NKJV). The key to quality of life, success, and overcoming stress is *love*.

In an intensive Harvard study spanning over seventy years, George Vaillant summarizes that "the only thing that really matters in life are your relationships to other people."[11] So in all the places in the Bible where we are instructed to love God and to love one another, it turns out God is giving us the key to overcoming hardships and living a happy, healthy life. Isolation is the devil's tool; he loves for you to pull away from your social group, and he laughs when you give your friends and family the cold shoulder, because it gives him the foothold he needs to get you to slip into depression by allowing the wrong chemicals in your body to prosper while depleting you of the chemicals God created to be excreted when we have social contact. Isolation is deadly, and Scripture and science prove we are better together.

## INVITATION TO PRAYER

Lord, thank you for all the relationships in my life, especially my relationship with you. Help me to love people well, and to build bridges of communication, social activities, and problem-solving. Thank you for calling us to be a part of a church—a community of prayer, worship, discipleship, service, and fellowship where I can love and be loved. Show me people in my daily life who need a friend; give me mentors and people I can grow with through the tough and triumphant days of life.

# DAY 53

# WEDNESDAY: WISDOM

*And not only this, but we also exult in our tribulations, knowing that tribulation brings about perseverance; and perseverance, proven character; and proven character, hope; and hope does not disappoint, because the love of God has been poured out within our hearts through the Holy Spirit who was given to us.*

ROMANS 5:3–5

Jesus never promised to keep pain and problems out of our lives, but he did promise to be our strength through them. We tend to want to avoid the hard days, but our testimonies are written on the pages of painful trials and how God amazingly sustains us with his hope and help. He may bring healing, funding, or restoration, but even when things do not turn out like we prayed or planned, his comfort and strength provide something new in us; our faith grows to new levels preparing us for something better.

My son, Chandler, was diagnosed with a rare blood cancer when he was a junior in high school. Chandler's surprising response to the doctor was, "Either way I win." He continued to explain that if, through the miracle of medication, God allowed the doctor to cure him and he had more time on earth, that was a win; but if God decided to take him to heaven through the illness, then he would get to be with Jesus, and that was definitely a win! How could a sixteen-year-old respond this way? Chandler says it was because of the prior fourteen-year journey through my brain tumor. He had seen and experienced all of the opportunities we had to express our faith and strengthen others. He took those lessons and applied them to his current situation; he saw this as an opportunity to glorify God, not question or curse him.

Stop dulling or dodging the pain of your circumstances and know that wisdom comes from walking through it with God. Know that tribulation in our life will bring about perseverance, prove our character, and result in hope.

## INVITATION TO PRAYER

Lord, help me to remember to cling to you when I am walking through the rough waves of life and start to get that sinking feeling. Problems come with your promise of growing us and greater days. Wisdom is not hiding from the trial but trusting you and looking for the opportunities to glorify you through it.

# DAY 54

# THURSDAY: HAPPINESS

*It is good for me that I was afflicted,*
*That I may learn Your statutes.*
*The law of Your mouth is better to me*
*Than thousands of gold and silver pieces.*

PSALM 119:71-72

Have you ever gone through something terrible and run around telling people, "Wow, I am so happy that I suffered!" Have you ever gone to visit a friend who is recovering from deep pain or dark times only to have them exclaim, "I am so happy I went through that!"

That is exactly what we are hearing from the psalmist; the word *good* translated from the Hebrew word *towb* means to be joyful, pleasant, right, and happy.[12] The word *afflicted* is translated from the Hebrew word *anah* and it means oppressed, depressed, put low, humbled.[13] Basically he is saying that it was right or he is happy to have been hurt, harmed, and/or humbled because God used it to teach him lessons about God that are more valuable than gold or silver.

The most valuable lesson might be to learn how to choose to stay happy through the process knowing the pain will end in gain. How can we keep our eye on the prize and not the pain? By keeping our eyes on God. Seeking his face before his favor and desiring the lesson over comfort. God's good for you is more valuable than gold; affliction is an asset if your heart and mind are focused on the teacher and trust that there is kingdom opportunity for his glory and your growth in earthly tests and trials. Don't quit! In life, you have to pass the test, cross the finish line, and finish a level in a video game to move on to the next level; you don't get a reward and move forward when you fail to finish. Stop focusing on the pain and be embraced by happiness, knowing treasure is in the trial.

## INVITATION TO PRAYER

Lord, I choose happiness in the trials of life, knowing you teach me and so I can reach new levels of love and life in you. Let your happiness overflow in my heart so that my mouth is filled with gratefulness for lessons learned along painful paths. Lift my face and keep my mouth filled with praise. I treasure your lessons and walk through them in your love.

# DAY 55

# FRIDAY: PURPOSE

*"I have said these things to you, that in me you may have peace.
In the world you will have tribulation. But take heart; I have
overcome the world."*

JOHN 16:33 ESV

It is always disheartening to hear people get angry or even blame God when pain and suffering occur. The idea of *How could a loving God allow good people to suffer?* does not seem like a logical question. After all, Christianity began and salvation was extended when a perfect, sinless man suffered unimaginable pain at the hands of man. And the Father allowed this so his wrath was satisfied and heaven's gates would swing open to those who believed and called him Lord.

Many of the psalms were penned when David was suffering, running for his life, and living in caves, with his enemies surrounding him and his family deserting him. Yet, in the midst of suffering, David cried out to God and then penned praise and thanks, knowing God's purposes would prevail. Beyond this notion, David understood that whether the trial was discipline from God or an attempt on his life from the devil, God would play out the situation for David's good and God's glory.

Stop chasing a pain-free existence and be embraced by the overcoming power and purposes of God. He never promised to take the trials out of our lives, but he did promise to take them on for us and with us.

## INVITATION TO PRAYER

Lord, I know that some pain is discipline; when we sin you allow it to hurt us, for there to be consequences such as in the story of the prodigal son, so that we will come to our senses and return to you. Other times, we get caught in the crossfire of other people's sin; our decisions always touch the lives of others, they are never isolated. Hardship can be the result of the brokenness of this world—disease, natural disasters, mental illness, and hate. Show me when my pain is a result of my sin. Search me that I may repent if I have been letting sin thrive in my life. If not, then I ask you to teach me as I trust you through these days of pain so that your purpose and glory prevail. Assure me through your presence and purposes as your good overcomes the trials and tribulations of life.

# DAY 56

# SATURDAY: SELAH ... PAUSE AND PONDER

## REVIEW

As you take time to pause and ponder all that you have read this week, set aside a few minutes to reread the verses from the previous six days. As you meditate on these verses, choose one to write down and memorize; let it become the truth that replaces the wrong thinking that you have thrown in the trash. Every time you catch yourself believing and repeating the lie, stop immediately and be embraced with truth by reading or reciting this passage.

## RECORD

Write down in your journal or notebook at least one specific lesson you learned this week that touched your heart and began to transform your thinking. Commit to making it a habit to review and include it in your prayer time. Be still and allow God to embrace you with the desires of your heart.

Praise him in his attributes that strengthen your faith, and thank him for the hope and help that can only come from knowing him in clearer and nearer ways this week.

## Respond

Make a one- to two-sentence plan of how you will apply this lesson in your life—at home, at work, and in the ways you think and act toward yourself and others. Allow the Holy Spirit to prompt you and provide the courage, humility, love, and anything else you might need to embrace righteous thinking and Christlike character.

## Invitation to Prayer

Lord, your Word says, "When the righteous cry for help, the LORD hears and delivers them out of all their troubles" (Psalm 34:17 ESV). In my troubles I cry out to you knowing that I can experience peace in your shelter and wisdom through the pain. Strengthen me to run to you and to friends and family; do not let me isolate myself in pity or pride. Let others see my faith and draw nearer to you. Assure me of your love. Search and show me if I have sinned against you so that I can repent and restore tranquility between us and in my circumstances. Give me the courage to move forward in tribulation, for your lessons are to make me better not battered. Let steadfastness be a part of my character and happiness mark my shield that faces pain straight on, knowing it is well with my soul.

# DAY 57

# SUNDAY: FOCUSED AND FOUND IN GOD

*The sower sows the word. These are the ones who are beside the road where the word is sown; and when they hear, immediately Satan comes and takes away the word which has been sown in them. ... On whom seed was sown on the rocky places, who, when they hear the word, immediately receive it with joy; and they have no firm root in themselves, but are only temporary; then, when affliction or persecution arises because of the word, immediately they fall away. And others ... seed was sown among the thorns; these are the ones who have heard the word, but the worries of the world, and the deceitfulness of riches, and the desires for other things enter in and choke the word, and it becomes unfruitful. And those are the ones on whom seed was sown on the good soil; and they hear the word and accept it and bear fruit, thirty, sixty, and a hundredfold.*

MARK 4:14–20

The Word of God is planted in the soil of hearts. Hearts are being prepared and repaired all over the world. Everyone should submit to his turning over the dry and depleted topsoil to bring up the rich soil underneath filled with nutrients, ready to receive the seed of his Word throughout life. If we fight him, then our hearts become rocky places where the seed scatters and is easily stolen or blown away by worry and the world. God's hand and heart are tender toward the heart he prepares.

He is the Lord of the harvest. This week we will focus on the fact that God spoke the seed of his Word and created the heart where it is planted, therefore he alone knows every step that must be taken from plowing to planting, watering to pruning, and finally to a fruitful harvest. He equips us to be loving laborers to nurture what only he can grow.

## Invitation to Prayer

Lord, this is your field, seed, and soil. Thank you for allowing me to sow your Word, not my opinions. And thank you for the stories of your love and work in my life. Help me to realize that I have a new story each day with you; you are always blessing, always working, always with me. Give me courage as I remember that your Spirit is the one who convicts, calls, and carries hearts to you for the harvest.

# DAY 58

# MONDAY: PEACE

*But the wisdom from above is first pure, then peaceable, gentle, reasonable, full of mercy and good fruits, unwavering, without hypocrisy. And the seed whose fruit is righteousness is sown in peace by those who make peace.*

JAMES 3:17–18

This book is written to connect with the way God created us. A person must feel safe (peace) and then cared for or have a sense of *belonging* (love) before the brain switches on to ask itself, *What can I learn?* As you seek to share the love and message of Jesus, help people feel safe and cared for so they can open their hearts and minds to the message of salvation.

The first step of planting is plowing—digging up hard soil to prepare it to receive the seeds. Only God plows with sharp tools that pierce and break apart the soil caked in a painful past, pride, prejudice, and misused power. In seasons of plowing, we are called to tend to hearts with prayer and care. We must intercede before we seed.

Jesus came to separate the spirit from the flesh, to redeem the soul and life he designed for us. When you encounter someone who is being *plowed* with the sword of God's Word, the Spirit's conviction, or the painful consequences of sinful choices, they need us to feed the spirit, not comfort or coddle the flesh. Encourage the eternal. We do not want to judge and push people away during the plowing process, nor do we want to undo God's plowing by pushing and packing the soil back down, covering up the places God was revealing and redeeming.

Prayer also prepares you to share God's seeds from his Word for his harvest.

# INVITATION TO PRAYER

Lord, I love you. Thank you for the precious opportunities to sow the seeds of your Word. Please prepare me—plow through any hard places in my heart and remove any rocks that could trip me or be seen as hypocrisy. Remove my preferences and opinions, and rip judgment from me. I want to come boldly but not brashly; I want to be your instrument to show how others can have peace *with* you and *in* you. Prompt me to pray as you plow the soil of hearts and prepare them to receive your Word. Send me with a pure heart to those you have prepared.

# DAY 59

# TUESDAY: LOVE

*Sow righteousness for yourselves,*
*reap the fruit of unfailing love,*
*and break up your unplowed ground;*
*for it is time to seek the LORD,*
*until he comes*
*and showers his righteousness on you.*

HOSEA 10:12 NIV

Today's verse teaches that love is reaped as we sow in righteousness. We encounter various reactions and emotions from people as God plows the hard soil in their hearts, and we must be prepared to respond in love. Our judgment does not bring people closer to God, and many times it pushes them farther away. Love draws people to feel safe and stick around to listen.

You may encounter the emotional rage of a heart split open as a harmful relationship is revealed or love is stolen away in sin. You may get caught in the crossfire of the mental agony of a divided mind that knows what it ought, but is addicted, attached, or just too lazy to do what is needed. Someone may try to pull you into the pain of unforgiveness, refusing to let go and let God heal the hurt so they can move forward in freedom. The physical brokenness of self-harm, lack of self-control, pride, insecurity, and loss are a fork in their path, where they either submit to God's work and love in their life to be changed forever or tragically fight and refuse God and continue to be chained to pain.

Sow prayer, truth, discipleship, and justice. Seek to do what is right until God's righteousness is revealed. Use what God has given you to show his love as you share from his Word. Be the example—God's visual aid of Jesus' love—willing to sow and grow his love in the lives of others.

## INVITATION TO PRAYER

Lord, thank you for plowing away the hard places in my heart and planting your love. Continue to show me where I need to grow, pull the weeds of sin out by the root, and nurture your fruit in my life. Let my life overflow toward others with the love and patience you have shown to me. Show me the needs that you would have me meet without interfering with the work you are doing. Shield and protect me as shots of pain fly from the lives and lips of others. Let love be my weapon to fight for them and not against them.

# DAY 60

# WEDNESDAY: WISDOM

*So neither the one who plants nor the one who waters is anything, but only God, who makes things grow. The one who plants and the one who waters have one purpose, and they will each be rewarded according to their own labor. For we are co-workers in God's service; you are God's field.*

1 CORINTHIANS 3:7–9 NIV

Wisdom waters and nurtures with the Word and love of God. It mentors without damaging new growth, guiding like a lattice for people to lean on to grow higher and stronger. We simply get to be a part of the process in God's service as he causes growth in his time, his way, and his field.

Our job description contains words and phrases like *pray, unite, peacemaker, dwell in unity with our brothers and sisters, love our enemies, share God's Word, be light,* and many others throughout each day, as people are getting to know and grow in their relationship with Jesus. Sowing God's Word is not a "one and done" responsibility; we should share his

Word with people every day, strengthening and discipling one another as we grow together.

We work through difficult lessons together such as forgiveness, loss, and knowing bad things do happen to good and godly people. Do not be like Job's not-so-wise friend who misjudged Job in his time of pain and said, "According to what I have seen, those who plow iniquity and those who sow trouble harvest it" (Job 4:8). While this may be true for those who sow trouble, it does not mean that every person experiencing pain caused it or deservedly had it coming. Satan was behind Job's troubles, and God had allowed it to prove Job's faithfulness, then "the LORD blessed Job's latter days more than his former ones" (Job 42:12 CEB). The *more* did not erase the mourning, but Job's faithfulness still inspires us thousands of years later.

## INVITATION TO PRAYER

Lord, thank you for your wisdom that waters the hearts of those who receive your Word and desire to grow in your glory. Thank you for teaching us, for sending mentors to us, for giving us new opportunities to grow our faith and see your power. Thank you that I have experienced your faithfulness. I will share my testimony of your greatness with others and pray that we know you more and more each day.

We have experienced your faithfulness. May we share our testimony of greatness with others + pray we know you know you more each day

# DAY 61

# THURSDAY: HAPPINESS

*Light is sown like seed for the righteous*
*And gladness for the upright in heart.*
*Be glad in the LORD, you righteous ones,*
*And give thanks to His holy name.*

PSALM 97:11–12

Yes, I will take this moment to say that everyone needs daily Son-shine. Go ahead, roll your eyes and groan at me for saying it, but it is true. We don't just need some vitamin D and fresh air; we need Jesus and all the love, grace, and compassion that he modeled in his ministry and poured out on the cross.

When a seed germinates, the hard shell is broken by the pressure created by heat of the soil and water. After the seed breaks open, the root grows first, seeking nutrients, and then the sprout bursts forth reaching upward for light. When the Sword separates flesh from Spirit, it is not our job to be salt in the wound but light in their darkness so that they grow toward God.

The same is true for discipleship, the journey of growth throughout our life as Christ followers. We need to take care and grow toward the light. Neuroscience researcher Alex Korb writes, "Everything is interconnected. Gratitude improves sleep. Sleep reduces pain. Reduced pain improves your mood. Improved mood reduces anxiety, which improves focus and planning. Focus and planning help with decision making. Decision making further reduces anxiety and improves enjoyment. Enjoyment gives you more to be grateful for, which keeps that loop of the upward spiral going. Enjoyment also makes it more likely you'll exercise and be social, which, in turn, will make you happier."[14] How many of these things have you done today? God created us so that healthy and happy routines support each other as we wrap each day in prayer, his Word, and loving people.

## Invitation to Prayer

Lord, you created us to be light and to grow in your light, not be anchored in darkness growing the wrong way deeper into darkness. I will reach for your light, in the godly, happy rhythms you created in me. Let my attitude be filled with gratitude to you and set the pace for me to think, say, and do all that you designed me to, always abiding in you. Let your righteousness be the gladness in our hearts.

# DAY 62

# FRIDAY: PURPOSE

*Seeing the people, He felt compassion for them, because they were distressed and dispirited like sheep without a shepherd. Then He said to His disciples, "The harvest is plentiful, but the workers are few. Therefore beseech the Lord of the harvest to send out workers into His harvest."*

MATTHEW 9:36–38

The idea of sharing a testimony or the plan of salvation frightens some people, but we are all called to make disciples, to show and share the love and message of Jesus. It becomes much easier when you realize what you are and are not responsible for. God is the Lord of the harvest; it is his field, his people that he created, his sacrifice and resurrection power that enables salvation, and his Spirit that convicts the heart, changes the heart, and produces fruit to his glory. We are not capable of or responsible for doing any of those things. If someone rejects the gospel, rejects our story of God's work in our life and pushes away the Bible for their own opinions, that is not on us. God will continue to draw them until their last breath. It is our responsibility to pray, to care, and to share the good news of Jesus in his Word and in our life.

We share our stories and Scripture with everyone, not just the lost. We are disciples—students who continue to learn every day. We are called to make disciples, not decision makers, to join us as lifelong learners and followers of Jesus. Accepting Jesus as Lord and Savior is the beginning of the journey, not the end. The relationship is only the beginning, just like a wedding is the beginning of a marriage.

The Spirit will equip you with examples and wisdom for your conversations. As you yield to him, he produces fruit in your life that gives God glory and shares more of the story.

## INVITATION TO PRAYER

Heavenly Father, I was born to know you and make you known. I am a laborer in your field. I understand that those who come to help plant or bring in the harvest know that what is brought in is not from their hand or for them to possess. They are only servants to bring in the harvest to the barn of the one who planted, watered, guarded, and nurtured the field from seed to fruit. Thank you for equipping me to labor with love.

# DAY 63

# SATURDAY: SELAH ... PAUSE AND PONDER

## REVIEW

As you take time to pause and ponder all that you have read this week, set aside a few minutes to reread the verses from the previous six days. As you meditate on these verses, choose one to write down and memorize; let it become the truth that replaces the wrong thinking that you have thrown in the trash. Every time you catch yourself believing and repeating the lie, stop immediately and be embraced with truth by reading or reciting this passage.

## RECORD

Write down in your journal or notebook at least one specific lesson you learned this week that touched your heart and began to transform your thinking and your behavior. Commit to making it a habit to review and include it in your prayer time. Be still and allow God to embrace you with the desires of your heart. Praise him in his attributes that strengthen your faith, and thank him for the hope and help that can only come from knowing him in clearer and nearer ways this week.

# RESPOND

Make a one- to two-sentence plan of how you will apply this lesson in your life—at home, at work, and in the ways you think and act toward yourself and others. Allow the Holy Spirit to prompt you and provide the courage, humility, love, and anything else you might need to embrace righteous thinking and Christlike character.

# INVITATION TO PRAYER

Lord, thank you for sowing your Word in my heart and growing me from plow to fruit. It is to your glory that I bear much fruit, and I know it is your Spirit that produces the fruit. I remain in you, abiding in your Word and ways that give life. Thank you for calling me to be a loving laborer, not a plowman with a blade but with prayer and care for those you set in my path. I am growing, not completed but in process. Help me to be patient with others who are growing, discipling them with the wisdom of your Word and the light of your blessings and faithfulness. (Pause and think of someone who does not know Jesus as their Lord and ask him to prepare their hearts for his Word, then pray for someone who is hurting and ask God how you can help them.) Lord, I am still growing. Please send mentors and teachers to help me.

# DAY 64

# SUNDAY: FOCUSED AND FOUND IN GOD

*The law of the LORD is perfect,*
*refreshing the soul.*
*The statutes of the LORD are trustworthy,*
*making wise the simple.*
*The precepts of the LORD are right,*
*giving joy to the heart.*
*The commands of the LORD are radiant,*
*giving light to the eyes.*
*The fear of the LORD is pure,*
*enduring forever.*
*The decrees of the LORD are firm,*
*and all of them are righteous.*
*They are more precious than gold,*
*than much pure gold.*

PSALM 19:7–10 NIV

The greatest asset, strength, and wisdom that you could ever store up in your life is the Word of God. For thousands of years before you were born, God was speaking into Scripture exactly what you would need for your next week, workday, conversation, decision, and relationship. God's Word brings refreshment to your innermost parts, all that you are is fueled by the One who knit you together. Fill up your thoughts with his thoughts; quit running on empty and guessing your way through. Use the righteous and trustworthy wisdom and warnings you store up as you read, study, and practice his words.

Do you look in the mirror and think, *I look so tired?* Spend some time resting and reading your Bible. Let the light it brings to your heart, spread to your eyes making you radiant with peace and joy. Let it be the light to your path and to his presence. Filling up and storing up God's information, instructions, and inspiration gives you an overflow of answers and affection, courage and compassion that is required of you. Store up truth and treasure it.

## INVITATION TO PRAYER

Lord, many days I come to you empty. Thank you for filling me. Your Word refreshes me; my soul soaks in your Word, and it heals my hurting heart. I want to store up your Word—for it to be as familiar as my favorite song that makes me feel happy to sing and that I know every word of. I want to meditate on your Word so your Spirit will grow it in my memory and mouth, replacing the thoughts or words that distract or even destroy. I want to be built up on the solid rock of your love, Word, and will. You are my source and my salvation.

# DAY 65

# MONDAY: PEACE

*So do not worry, saying, "What shall we eat?" or "What shall we drink?" or "What shall we wear?" For the pagans run after all these things, and your heavenly Father knows that you need them. But seek first his kingdom and his righteousness, and all these things will be given to you as well. Therefore do not worry about tomorrow, for tomorrow will worry about itself. Each day has enough trouble of its own.*

MATTHEW 6:31–34 NIV

Peace comes when you stop defining wealth as *mine*, but *thine*, which is the archaic word for *yours*. Everything you have comes from God. Yes, you work hard to earn the money but God gave you the life, the ability to learn and work, the opportunity to interview and get the job—you get the picture. God has blessed you with all you have, and he has the power to multiply it when you serve him with it, but he could take it even quicker than he gave it if you let it get between your relationship and love for him.

A mind set on seeking God does not have time or space for worry. Peace increases when worry decreases; peace will permeate a heart that has not made room for anxiety. Faith says, *God knows what I need, and I have prayed and asked with a pure heart and so now I will wait in peace while God determines and distributes the blessings of each day.* Peace knows God, seeks and trusts him, and therefore peace is stored up and pours out to extinguish worry when it tries to distract or derail you.

Embrace God's invitation to prayer, and be embraced by the peace of knowing "Whoever pursues righteousness and love finds life, prosperity and honor" (Proverbs 21:21 NIV).

## INVITATION TO PRAYER

Heavenly Father, thank you for feeding the birds and clothing lilies with your splendor and for knowing and supplying my needs. I will seek you to store up your Word and your love in my heart. I reject worry—it does not store up but breaks down, it wastes time, and it strains relationships and drains away my health and life. Fill and keep me in perfect peace, as I set my mind and trust steadfastly on you.

# DAY 66

# TUESDAY: LOVE

*But store up for yourselves treasures in heaven, where moths and vermin do not destroy, and where thieves do not break in and steal. For where your treasure is, there your heart will be also.*

MATTHEW 6:20–21 NIV

What do you think of when you hear the word *treasure*? Do you picture a chest filled with gold, pearls, gems, and ancient items? Do you think of a bank vault or a home safe where you keep money or papers that prove ownership of insurance and investments? Do you connect it with assets like your home or property? Scripture says that you can map a person's treasure by looking at what is at the center of their physical and spiritual life. The *heart* is seen as the "fountain and seat of the thoughts, passions, desires, appetites, affections, purposes, endeavors."[15]

If you spend a majority of your time, passion, talent, and energy on making money, if you stay awake at night thinking about it or it is one of your first thoughts in the morning, then money marks the *X* on the map to your heart. Remember, peace comes when you realize what money is *for* not when you are obsessed with more. Love lives when you learn to give. A heart that is laying up treasure in heaven is more excited about giving resources away than storing them. I am not talking about having money in savings or a college fund for your children—we will discuss that later this week—but you can know where your treasure is by the affection and attention you give it and the affirmation you get from it. We should love people, not money.

Stop chasing earthly wealth and be embraced by the riches of love and generosity. Loving people is the greatest long-term investment you can make, and in Christ the returns are eternal.

## INVITATION TO PRAYER

Lord, you are my love. I desire to love you with *all* my heart, soul, mind, and strength—do not let money embezzle my love. You have said that the love of money is the root of all kinds of evil (1 Timothy 6:10 NIV); please pull that root if it is in my heart. I want the resources you give to pour through me, not be stored for just me. Teach me how to use money as a tool to show and share your love.

# DAY 67

# WEDNESDAY: WISDOM

*My son, if you accept my words
and store up my commands within you,
turning your ear to wisdom
and applying your heart to understanding—
indeed, if you call out for insight
and cry aloud for understanding,
and if you look for it as for silver
and search for it as for hidden treasure,
then you will understand the fear of the LORD
and find the knowledge of God.*

PROVERBS 2:1–5 NIV

Wisdom is an absolute necessity when it comes to managing money. In the parable of the talents found in Matthew 25:14–30, we see the reward that comes to the servant who earnestly invests what has been entrusted to him by his master. The money was greatly multiplied in the hands of the wise. The wicked servant hid it in the ground, did not even put it in the bank to gain interest. In today's standards, this money would have been worth millions of dollars. Jesus was clearly making a point about using and investing what God has entrusted to us; having money is not evil, *loving* money is.

More valuable than silver or any other treasure, wisdom is the *what* we call out for when we are seeking God and his righteousness. If we store up God's words and commands in our life, then the wisdom obtained walking with God will manage and multiply it in our lives. If you want the giver more than the gift, the Father more than the favor, then you are storing up wisdom more valuable than any other wealth.

This week's verses have used words and phrases like *seek*, *cry out*, and *search*. It is obvious that our relationship with Jesus is not a casual friendship; we must be tenacious in our relationship with the One who designed us and our days, and store up all the wisdom he gives for us to manage and make the most of our life and treasure.

## INVITATION TO PRAYER

Lord Jesus, more than anything I want to know you. I seek you and search for your wisdom as a treasure more valuable than anything on earth. I need wisdom in my life, my relationships, my decisions, my family, and all the things I do not know or understand. Store up your Word in my heart so that it fills my mind and overflows from my lips; embrace me with your wisdom.

# DAY 68

# THURSDAY: HAPPINESS

*No one can serve two masters. Either you will hate the one and love the other, or you will be devoted to the one and despise the other. You cannot serve both God and money.*

MATTHEW 6:24 NIV

Money cannot buy happiness. I know you might be laughing right now as you think, *Well, I would like to see for myself.* The truth is, if you do not learn the correct mindset about money, it will make you miserable as it becomes your master. The more wealth you have, the more time and resources it takes to manage, insure, protect, and keep it. You worry about losing it, someone stealing it, updating it to maintain its value—until it becomes an emotional roller coaster when it comes to spending it, and on and on it goes, costing you money and sleep in its service.

Happiness comes in the *stewardship*, not ownership of wealth. You may be thinking, *I am not wealthy,* but you are. In the year 2015, 71 percent of the world's population had total wealth of less than $10,000.[16] That included home, possessions, and income. This shifts our perspective from *I want more* to *I have more*. A grateful heart is a happy heart, and there is plenty of Scripture and science to back that up as well.

Happiness is stored up when God uses us to pour out his resources. Blessings tend to increase when our hands release. Happy hands and hearts open up to give and are lifted up in praise.

## INVITATION TO PRAYER

Lord, thank you for all that you have given to me, for sustaining me far beyond my needs. I know that I am blessed. All I have is yours; I will not compare myself to those who have more or less, but I will focus on what you call me to do with all that you have given to me. Thank you for the roof over my head, the fact that I can read this book, the food I have eaten today, and the clothes I am wearing. Show me where I can give. I will be faithful to tithe and not steal from you, and I will give where you show me, to people in need so they can see your love and be happy in you.

# DAY 69

# FRIDAY: PURPOSE

*Ants are creatures of little strength,*
*yet they store up their food in the summer;*
*hyraxes are creatures of little power,*
*yet they make their home in the crags.*

PROVERBS 30:25–26 NIV

Every day this week, we touched on the purpose and place of money in our lives. Money is a gift from God, a resource for us to use for his purposes, which include sustaining our lives. You did not hear me say that you should give everything away and not save for a rainy day. Today's verses cite two of the four things that are small but extremely wise on earth. The ant stores up food and the hyrax a safe place to live. The same is true for us—it is wise to save, to pay our bills, to send our kids to college, and to not have to rely on someone else in retirement or crisis. Peace trusts God and wisdom saves; it does not hoard or spend every penny we earn. Love knows that people are treasure and money is not. Peace and happiness give generously, first to God and then to meet the needs of others. Wisdom manages life, and money is only a part of our lives.

Money has purpose, but it is not your purpose. You were not given life to make a living—you work to live, not live to work. Money is a tool, a resource that can be used to share and show the love of God. You, your church, and other ministries can use it to care for those in need and to share the gospel around the world. Money is necessary, but without peace, love, wisdom, and happiness, it has no purpose. Stop chasing bigger and more, and be embraced by the purpose stored up for you in heaven.

## INVITATION TO PRAYER

Lord, thank you for your provision, for money that can be exchanged for the needs in our lives and be saved for the future needs you have shown us. Help me to count the cost of every purchase and decision, do not let money become my master, and keep me from becoming a slave to debt. I know I must be faithful to tithe to you—it shows my thanks for all that you have given—and I trust you'll provide for my needs. Let my treasure be stored in heaven.

# DAY 70

# SATURDAY: SELAH ... PAUSE AND PONDER

## REVIEW

As you take time to pause and ponder all that you have read this week, set aside a few minutes to reread the verses from the previous six days. As you meditate on these verses, choose one to write down and memorize; let it become the truth that replaces the wrong thinking that you have thrown in the trash. Every time you catch yourself believing and repeating the lie, stop immediately and be embraced with truth by reading or reciting this passage.

## RECORD

Write down in your journal or notebook at least one specific lesson you learned this week that touched your heart and began to transform your thinking. Commit to making it a habit to review and include it in your prayer time. Be still and allow God to embrace you with the desires of your heart.

Praise him in his attributes that strengthen your faith, and thank him for the hope and help that can only come from knowing him in clearer and nearer ways this week.

## Respond

Make a one- to two-sentence plan of how you will apply this lesson in your life—at home, at work, and in the ways you think and act toward God, yourself, and others. Allow the Holy Spirit to prompt you and provide the courage, humility, love, and anything else you might need to embrace righteous thinking and Christlike character.

## Invitation to Prayer

Lord, I seek you and your righteousness, knowing that you will add to my life what I need, and I pray that you will take away anything that displeases you. Your peace, love, wisdom, happiness, and purpose are more valuable to me than any earthly earning. The people you have put in my life are my treasure, and my walk with you is my wealth. I want to store up eternal treasures and be a good steward of earthly blessings. All I have is from you and for you. Make changes in my attitude, affection, and actions with money; reckon my accounts with your purposes. Show me where to give, spend, and save; let me glorify you as a Christian who pays their bills on time and does not spend more than I earn. Do not let me cast this lesson aside; I know that loving you with my all includes my finances, and so I walk with you to get wisdom in my wealth both here and in heaven.

DAY 71

# SUNDAY: FOCUSED AND FOUND IN GOD

*Do not conform to the pattern of this world, but be transformed by the renewing of your mind. Then you will be able to test and approve what God's will is—his good, pleasing and perfect will.*

ROMANS 12:2 NIV

Have you ever heard the phrase *birds of a feather flock together*? It describes the idea that people who are alike form relationships. Interestingly, science is now saying that you begin to think and behave like the people you hang out with, even if you think you won't. Neuroscience research has found that when two people are in each other's company, their brain waves will begin to look nearly identical.[17] Proximity builds an alignment in brainwaves, first thoughts and eventually behaviors. This should prompt us to pause and seriously consider who we spend our time with. Psalm 1:1 says, "How blessed is the man who does not walk in the counsel of the wicked, nor stand in the path of sinners, nor sit in the seat of scoffers!"

Once again, God was saying it long before science proved it. You may start out believing that other people do not influence you, but Scripture and science disagree.

Spending time with God in prayer and studying his Word builds your relationship and is part of the process of being conformed to the mind and character of Christ. The more time you spend with Jesus, the more your thoughts, emotions, and actions will mirror his will. Jesus prayed his followers would be one; we are unified as we abide in Christ and with his followers. Unity does not take away our uniqueness; it completes us to know and walk in his will that is pleasing and perfectly designed for us in our unique situations, relationships, and where and when we live. Influence others toward God, and never let them pull you away from him.

## INVITATION TO PRAYER

Lord, I want to draw closer to you as you conform my character to align with your affection, actions, and attributes. I want the life that you have designed for me. Renew my mind and protect me from aligning with the patterns of this world and the worldly. I want to listen to you as you guide me and grow me, so keep me close and keep the enemy far away. Give me discernment to know who will help me and who will hurt me.

# DAY 72

# MONDAY: PEACE

*But He knew their thoughts and said to them,
"Any kingdom divided against itself is laid waste;
and a house divided against itself falls."*

LUKE 11:17

God created us for relationship; we need one another for numerous reasons. No man is an island. We need one another to survive and prosper, for love and fellowship both individually and as a nation.

Sadly, it seems that America today is divided in many ways. Our political views, personal preferences, religious traditions, pride, greed, and many other things have led to dispute and division that will not only affect families and friends but, as Jesus warned, will cause us to fall. In order to save America, we must pray for our country and act in love and unity toward one another. We will not have peace from our enemies if we cannot live in peace with one another. Satan and nations who oppose us laugh with delight when we collide and divide on the national stage; we must work out our differences privately so that we can work and walk united. Unity builds up our families, neighbors, the church, and America in ways that glorify God and move us forward in peace, prosperity, and even politics.

Take some time to think of the divided houses you may be a part of. How can you be a peacemaker with your influence? If you have been a part of the division, how can you work toward bringing back unity? Unity requires humility; it often requires apologies and it always requires self-control. Modeling control of your own desires sets the stage for peace and for others to follow. Stop the fight of being critical or complaining, and be embraced in the peace and unity that comes with humility and praise.

## INVITATION TO PRAYER

Lord Jesus, you created us to love one another. We are built up when we love, and peace spreads when we are humble and not hateful. You warned us that division will destroy us. Please bring peace—your peace—to our words and world. Heal our hearts and then heal our land by bringing us to our knees in our desperation for you and our desire to bring you glory. Let our nation be known as "one nation under God," let us live up to that motto and let it be a model for other nations to follow.

# DAY 73

# TUESDAY: LOVE

*Let no unwholesome word proceed from your mouth, but only such a word as is good for edification according to the need of the moment, so that it will give grace to those who hear. Do not grieve the Holy Spirit of God, by whom you were sealed for the day of redemption. Let all bitterness and wrath and anger and clamor and slander be put away from you, along with all malice. Be kind to one another, tender-hearted, forgiving each other, just as God in Christ also has forgiven you.*

EPHESIANS 4:29–32

In 2014 a research report was published titled "Matchmaking Promotes Happiness." I found this interesting because I looked at it with a *higher* point of view, not so much thinking about the matchmaking as much as the unifying that takes place when we bring people together. One of the theories noted in the research is that "bringing others together may signal one's status in the social network."[18] I stopped and wondered, *Could it really be a signal of our spiritual network?*—the physical response to the spiritual affection and activity of love.

We were made for love and relationships; Jesus prayed his disciples would be unified, so it makes sense that our

God-created bodies would be flooded with happiness when we bring people together. Our greatest happiness comes in introducing people to their greatest love, Jesus!

The world is so divided that our nation is tearing itself apart as we devour one another in our differences. We are surrounded by messages that darken and depress our emotions. God calls us to love one another, to be tender-hearted. Our words are supposed to edify and encourage, not tear down and tear apart.

## INVITATION TO PRAYER

Lord, I desire to be kind and tender-hearted. I want to love people as you love us, and I want to be a peacemaker. Please equip me in your love to overflow through my words and life to bring people together to know you, to worship and pray, to serve you and know you as their Lord. Let me seek out opportunities to introduce people—my friends and acquaintances—to one another so that your love might be their connecting point that expands into friendship, prayer partners, collaboration in service, and love for one another.

# DAY 74

# WEDNESDAY: WISDOM

*But now you yourselves are to put off all these: anger, wrath, malice, blasphemy, filthy language out of your mouth. Do not lie to one another, since you have put off the old man with his deeds, and have put on the new man who is renewed in knowledge according to the image of Him who created him, where there is neither Greek nor Jew, circumcised nor uncircumcised, barbarian, Scythian, slave nor free, but Christ is all and in all. Therefore, as the elect of God, holy and beloved, put on tender mercies, kindness, humility, meekness, longsuffering; bearing with one another, and forgiving one another, if anyone has a complaint against another; even as Christ forgave you, so you also must do. But above all these things put on love, which is the bond of perfection. And let the peace of God rule in your hearts, to which also you were called in one body; and be thankful.*

Colossians 3:8–15 NKJV

Are you stumped over bringing unity to a broken relationship or situation? Has something separated you from friends or family? Do you find yourself at odds with coworkers or even people who attend your church? Good news! Today's verses are filled with wisdom that brings unity; simply "dress for success." Okay, I am not talking about pulling a suit out of your closet; I am referring to the fact that as a Christ follower, you have *put off* the old self that was all about yourself and have now "put on the new man" or woman. The new you is renewed by the knowledge and image of God, the same image in which every person is created; it is our connecting point and the starting point for us to value every single person on earth. As you get ready for your day, thank God and pray through the "wardrobe" he has picked out for you.

## INVITATION TO PRAYER

Lord, as I prepare for today, I choose the smart look—the wardrobe of wisdom that you have designed for me. I put on tender mercies, kindness, humility, meekness, and longsuffering. You wrap me in forgiveness, therefore I will embrace others with forgiveness and will seek forgiveness with those who have a complaint against me; I will seek unity and to be a peacemaker. I know this all must be brought together with love—your love—that brings devotion instead of division.

# DAY 75

# THURSDAY: HAPPINESS

*Behold, how good and pleasant it is
when brothers dwell in unity!*

PSALM 133:1 ESV

God put an exclamation point at the end of this thought. It is a passionate declaration, as God explains once again how he created us to live and thrive. It is not just fun to do life together with others, it is essential. Disunity not only breaks down progress, but also breaks down processes in our brain and body, causing dysfunction and even disease. As study after study are published in books and medical journals, we know that unity and connectedness leads to healthier and longer lives.[19] I remind you that God does not need science to prove him right, but he has allowed science to confirm what Scripture says to help us when we share with people who do not believe the Bible or think that faith is for the weak minded. God's wisdom has been telling us for thousands of years what science is just catching up to see: we were made for love and unity.

Shawn Achor explains in his book *The Happiness Advantage* that a person's social network is key to their success through stress.[20] Unfortunately, we have been taught to isolate ourselves in times of challenge, deadlines, and exams, locking ourselves in our office or in a corner of the library, refusing to even break to go eat with others. Science tells us that we are better together; God made us to need others, and Jesus prayed that we, his disciples, would be one as he and the Father are one.

## INVITATION TO PRAYER

Lord, you are my help and happiness. Please quiet my mind from conflict and clutter, and help me to see where I have caused or participated in disunity. Show me where I have separated myself from people I can trust, who care about me, and have thoughts and knowledge that I need to live, learn, love, and work with success. I don't want pride or pressure to get in the way of my relationships. Help me press in with the community of people you have put in my life to share the collective education, experience, and emotions that you have given to us. Let us dwell in unity.

# DAY 76

# FRIDAY: PURPOSE

*But you are a chosen race, a royal priesthood, a holy nation, a people for his own possession, that you may proclaim the excellencies of him who called you out of darkness into his marvelous light.*

1 PETER 2:9 ESV

God chose you and made you his own, and as if that were not enough to keep you rejoicing, he made you a part of his holy people. The word *holy* here describes you as a saint, his sanctuary, separated from sin but not called to live separated from people. God chose you to bring light into darkness; your prayers invite him to intervene in sin and strife. He chose you to live differently but not divided. Because you are a citizen of his kingdom, you do not let culture form you but are chosen to transform it, to be a Christ-centered culture creator wherever you live, learn, hang out, work out, worship, and work. Because you belong and are beloved by Jesus, you get to experience all that God calls you to before he sends you out to express it. He does not ask you to do anything that he has not already done for you. It is personal before it is proclaimed, that is your testimony. All that Jesus has done for you is available to others.

Notice that you are a part of a holy nation, a people—it is plural. You are meant to be a part of something bigger than yourself, not to go it alone. It is why we identify with sports teams and community groups, regions and nationalities, and generations and the music or movements they represent, but most importantly we are to recognize and reflect our identity in Christ and serve the unity of the church, the royal priesthood that we are called into. How do you serve and bring unity to your church? Does your church participate in serving your community with other churches? How could you help perpetuate unity to serve, fill a need, or bring them together to pray?

## Invitation to Prayer

Lord, use me to bring unity to your church, to bring people together in prayer, worship, and love. Let our unity be inviting, drawing the lost and lonely to join us as your disciples. Thank you for choosing me, calling me, and caring for me. Let me share your love with saints and seekers.

## DAY 77

# SATURDAY: SELAH ... PAUSE AND PONDER

### REVIEW

As you take time to pause and ponder all that you have read this week, set aside a few minutes to reread the verses from the previous six days. As you meditate on these verses, choose one to write down and memorize; let it become the truth that replaces the wrong thinking that you have thrown in the trash. Every time you catch yourself believing and repeating the lie, stop immediately and be embraced with truth by reading or reciting this passage.

### RECORD

Write down in your journal or notebook at least one specific lesson you learned this week that touched your heart and began to transform what you believe and how you behave. Commit to making it a habit to review and include it in your prayer time. Be still and allow God to embrace you with his will and the desires of your heart. Praise him in his attributes that strengthen your faith, and thank him for the hope and help that can only come from knowing him in clearer and nearer ways this week.

## RESPOND

Make a one- to two-sentence plan of how you will apply this lesson in your life—at home, at work, and in the ways you think and act toward God, yourself, and others. Allow the Holy Spirit to prompt you and provide the courage, humility, love, and anything else you might need to be embraced by righteous thinking and Christlike character.

## INVITATION TO PRAYER

Heavenly Father, use me to influence your followers to be unified in our love, worship, and obedience to you. Unite us in love that spills out of our church doors and saturates our communities and nation. Let us be one nation under God, a family under God, lives lived in and under your authority and will. Align me with your Word and will, and put me in the path and lives of those who need you and your salvation, encouragement, strength, love, commands, and courage that give us abundant life. Thank you for protecting me from harm; keep me from running to it. Let me love people who don't know you, but protect me so I do not get detoured or distracted. Teach us to listen with love and lead others to you. Bring your followers together so that our love and fellowship draws others to follow you.

# DAY 78

# SUNDAY: FOCUSED AND FOUND IN GOD

*And Jesus came up and spoke to them, saying, "All authority has been given to Me in heaven and on earth. Go therefore and make disciples of all the nations, baptizing them in the name of the Father and the Son and the Holy Spirit, teaching them to observe all that I commanded you; and lo, I am with you always, even to the end of the age."*

MATTHEW 28:18–20

Jesus gave his disciples a commission with provision, to go and make disciples everywhere, baptizing them and teaching them in the authority he was giving them and the Spirit that would empower *all* of his disciples for all the ages until he returns.

I almost titled this week's theme "Called to Leadership," but real leadership involves discipleship. You must see your influence and relationships as God's opportunities to disciple people; to show them what it looks like to be a Christ follower; and to work and live with Christlike, God-obeying character and values. Whatever you do, wherever you are—at work or home, as members of clubs, teams, or organizations, and at church—you are called to disciple. A disciple is a pupil; after we ask Jesus to be our Lord and Savior, we become disciples, pupils of his Word, will, and ways. We are learners for a lifetime, not decision makers in a moment. Salvation is not a death-destination decision; it is a lifetime learning, loving, living decision that we do with others who need or know Jesus.

Do not orphan our newest family members after they receive Christ as their Savior; their prayer is the beginning of the journey, not the end. Learn together. You are a disciple called to make disciples and to discipleship throughout life. If you are a parent, remember that you are not just rearing children, but making disciples. Make prayer and teaching God's Word a part of your family time and time with friends, when you work and play and throughout your day.

## INVITATION TO PRAYER

Jesus, thank you for making me your disciple and commissioning me to go and make disciples. Empower me with your Spirit and compel me with your love. Teach me more and more each day so I can share your message and love as I am praying, caring, and sharing your Word and ways in the influence and relationships you provide. Remind me that the greatest leadership is discipleship.

# DAY 79

# MONDAY: PEACE

*The LORD is my shepherd;*
*I have all that I need.*
*He lets me rest in green meadows;*
*he leads me beside peaceful streams.*
*He renews my strength.*
*He guides me along right paths,*
*bringing honor to his name.*
*Even when I walk*
*through the darkest valley,*
*I will not be afraid,*
*for you are close beside me.*
*Your rod and your staff*
*protect and comfort me. ...*
*Surely your goodness and unfailing love will pursue me*
*all the days of my life.*

PSALM 23:1–4, 6 NLT

What do you think of when you hear the word *leader*? Do you get images of someone who is powerful, influential, or the decision maker that takes an idea or organization to where it needs to go or grow? Do you think of someone who is bossy or brave, gives opportunity or orders, is sacrificial or selfish? Your experiences and desires shape the way you think about things, but unfortunately, they may be *misleading* you.

In Psalm 23, we see that when God is our leader—our shepherd—he leads us to rest, resources, refreshment, renewal, righteousness, refuge, and respect. All of these provide peace in our lives. His peace guards, guides, and provides in all our circumstances. This is the right model for the type of leader we should aspire to be. Yes, you are a leader. Everyone has influence over at least one other person. Someone you work, live, learn, or play with looks up to you; they listen and watch your life for cues on how to live or improve their life. Lead and disciple others to something or somewhere that is better for them, not you. Be a safe place, a peace-filled leader that flows from the peace God gives to you. Stop chasing positions of power and be embraced by God to direct your path to people as you direct people to God.

## INVITATION TO PRAYER

Lord, thank you for being my shepherd, the one who leads me to peaceful and protected places. I want to stay under your authority as you give me opportunities to lead and disciple others. Show me how to be a peace-filled person even in the valleys of life so that those around me respond to your peace in me and through me. Guide me so I can guide others through you and to you.

# DAY 80

# TUESDAY: LOVE

*A new commandment I give to you, that you love one another,*
*even as I have loved you, that you also love one another.*
*By this all men will know that you are My disciples,*
*if you have love for one another.*

JOHN 13:34–35

Love is the key characteristic of being a disciple and making disciples. Jesus said his disciples would be recognized by their love, and science says you cannot teach someone until they feel safe and loved or have a sense of belonging. Love paves the way for discipleship and leadership. Jesus' love rises above all selfishness; it is a love that serves others first for the purpose and message of the kingdom.

In a *Harvard Business Review* article on emotional intelligence "What Makes a Leader," Daniel Goleman reveals that emotional intelligence is twice as important as IQ and technical skills when it comes to excellent performance and effective leadership.[21] Your mood, motivation, empathy, and emotional makeup wrapped in self-control are the characteristics that rise to the top of the leadership scale—and taking a closer in-depth look will show you that they are the fruit of the Spirit.

Love makes a good leader and a great disciple maker. You cannot share the gospel in understandable, receivable ways until a person feels safe and cared for when they are around you. Being a Lord-led leader, saturated in and showing Christ's love, will increase productivity, loyalty, and job satisfaction. Emotional intelligence is "not just a personal virtue but an organizational strength."[22] Let the Lord's love lead you.

## INVITATION TO PRAYER

Lord, thank you for loving me and for calling and commissioning your followers to share your love. Guide and guard us as we love one another. Prompt us to be disciples who love so that others will want to know you and become your disciples. I want to spend my life with others talking about your Word, how we worship, and what it means to walk in your love. Let me be recognized and characterized as your disciple by love.

# DAY 81

# WEDNESDAY: WISDOM

*[If] my people who are called by My name humble themselves and pray and seek My face and turn from their wicked ways, then I will hear from heaven, will forgive their sin and will heal their land.*

2 CHRONICLES 7:14

Perhaps you have heard this verse used during prayer for a nation. Its wisdom for us comes from reading it in context to what has just happened and understanding why God is giving these instructions and promise. In 2 Chronicles 7, King Solomon has just dedicated the house of God in Jerusalem, and Solomon prayed for God to hear the prayers of all who come to pray and to be glorified and pleased with the sacrifices and worship that take place there. As you will read tomorrow, the people of Israel were happy because of the right relationship their leaders had with God, but God reminds Solomon that neither a building nor a king will strengthen or sustain them. God says that the nation will only be blessed if his *people* remain, or repent and return, in obedience and worship of him alone. It is important to have a Jesus-following leader, but God says it's not one man or woman but *all* of his people who must be humble, pray, seek him, and repent of their sins before God blesses that nation.

As a Christ follower, your life leads your nation toward or away from God. Jesus, not the person you did or did not vote for in an election, is your Savior. A godly leader can make a nation happy, but they do not make it holy. Every Christian is commanded to live according to God's ways even when sin is considered legal. Christ, not culture, gives us the wisdom leading to peace and prosperity that only comes from pleasing God. Stop chasing culture and start shaping it; pray for your nation as you are embraced by God's love and leadership.

## INVITATION TO PRAYER

Jesus, remind us that we are called by your name; you called us to love you, love one another, and make disciples. Let us be mindful of our own sin and repent from our own wicked ways that impede your healing and blessings in our own lives and our nation. Open our eyes, hearts, and hands to serve you and share your love, knowing you restore us. Jesus, you alone are my Lord and Savior.

# DAY 82

# THURSDAY: HAPPINESS

*Then on the twenty-third day of the seventh month he sent the people to their tents, rejoicing and happy of heart because of the goodness that the LORD had shown to David and to Solomon and to His people Israel.*

2 CHRONICLES 7:10

As I hinted to you yesterday, it makes people happy to have godly leaders. In these verses we see Israel rejoicing with happy hearts because of the Lord's goodness shown to David and Solomon. A leader that loves and worships the Lord will be a pipeline of blessing not only for himself or herself but also for those they live, work, and serve with. In addition, the people they lead experience a sense of care and confidence that their home, business, school district, government office, military squadron, etc. is being run with integrity and excellence.

What leadership skills and qualities have you experienced that you work to imitate in your areas of discipleship? Consider starting a list of qualities you find in Scripture and then ask God to develop these characteristics in your life and leadership. Pray regularly for the leaders in your life, from the president and other national leaders to members of your family, teams, church, work, and schools.

You may have just stopped and thought something like *You have got to be kidding me!* or *I don't agree with a single thing that woman (or man) says or does!* The truth is that it does not matter if you agree with them; God commands you to pray for them. Pray if you really want to see a change in their lives and leadership—if you want your nation, workplace, home, etc. to flourish and be a place of God's glory and happiness. Pray that God will intervene in their lives and that his presence will permeate their decisions, conversations, and actions. You will be deeply happy to see God work in their hearts and yours.

## INVITATION TO PRAYER

Lord Jesus, thank you for godly leaders who love and obey you, who put their trust in you and do the righteous thing even when it is not popular. Make me the kind of disciple maker that spreads your blessings, and fill my heart with happiness. I know that you are always my Lord and leader. May your power and glory flood our hearts and fill the earth.

# DAY 83

# FRIDAY: PURPOSE

*If I then, your Lord and Teacher, have washed your feet, you*
*also ought to wash one another's feet. For I have given you an*
*example, that you also should do just as I have done to you.*
*Truly, truly, I say to you, a servant is not greater than his master,*
*nor is a messenger greater than the one who sent him. If you*
*know these things, blessed are you if you do them.*

JOHN 13:14–17 ESV

Discipleship loves God and others in many ways. We show
love in our prayer life by studying the Bible and living in obedience to God, and through work and worship that respond
to God's love for us. Jesus said, "If you love Me, you will
keep My commandments" (John 14:15). We have been commanded to love and to make disciples. In every breath you face
decisions—how you will act, react, forgive. Do the right thing
even if it hurts your bottom line; puts your job at risk; or sets
you apart from the culture of your community, campus, or
workplace. "We ought to obey God rather than men" (Acts
5:29 NKJV). It is in obeying God that we serve mankind well,
with love and humility that Jesus showed when he took the
position of the lowest servant and washed the disciples' feet.

We need to act humbly to be happy, and to love in order to lead. Jesus says that he has *shown* us what to do, and blessed (happy) are we if we do those things. Sadly, even sinfully, some would rather judge the people we are sent to serve and love—people who do not know what they are supposed to do. Our attitude of judgment says, *I am greater than my master, greater than Jesus.* That should make you shudder and humble you to be ready and willing to wash feet, to serve and not be served, to disciple and love them instead of lord over them.

## INVITATION TO PRAYER

Jesus, you humbled yourself, coming from heaven fully God to earth to be fully man. You ministered and modeled love and the kingdom message, and sent out your disciples to spread this to the ends of the earth. Your message still spreads today, and I want to be your humble servant and messenger. Help me to remember that those who do not know you do not know your ways. They cannot be held to a standard they have never encountered or heard, so use me as your visual and voice to help them experience your love.

# DAY 84

# SATURDAY: SELAH ... PAUSE AND PONDER

## REVIEW

As you take time to pause and ponder all that you have read this week, set aside a few minutes to reread the verses from the previous six days. As you meditate on these verses, choose one to write down and memorize; let it become the truth that replaces the wrong thinking that you have thrown in the trash. Every time you catch yourself believing and repeating the lie, stop immediately and be embraced with truth by reading or reciting this passage.

## RECORD

Write down in your journal or notebook at least one specific lesson you learned this week that touched your heart and began to transform your thinking and behavior. Commit to making it a habit to review and include it in your prayer time. Be still and allow God to embrace you with the desires of your heart to share his love and message. Praise him in his attributes that strengthen your faith, and thank him for the hope and help that can only come from knowing him in clearer and nearer ways this week. Ask him to help you, to connect you with others, to be a disciple who studies God's Word and ways, and to be a disciple maker who shares Jesus' love and message.

## RESPOND

Make a one- to two-sentence plan of how you will apply this lesson in your life—at home, at work, and in the ways you think and act toward God, yourself, and others. Allow the Holy Spirit to prompt you and provide the courage, humility, love, and anything else you might need to be embraced by righteous thinking and Christlike character.

## INVITATION TO PRAYER

Jesus, you are my shepherd, my Lord, and the reason I live and am loved. Please forgive me for the times that I judged others instead of loving and discipling them. Please forgive me for putting myself above them and, even worse, for putting myself on the throne of judgment that God alone occupies. I am your disciple, your student; teach me every day. I know I have so much to learn, and I yearn for your Word to fill and guide my life. Help me to see that I do not need courage but humility to make disciples, to step into the opportunities you put in my life and sow your Word in the hearts you've prepared.

# DAY 85

# SUNDAY: FOCUSED AND FOUND IN GOD

*He who dwells in the shelter of the Most High
will abide in the shadow of the Almighty.
I will say to the LORD, "My refuge and my fortress,
my God, in whom I trust."*

PSALM 91:1–2 ESV

As we come to the last week of this devotional journey, it will be essential for you to continue to abide in the embrace of the Almighty and to continue to exercise all that you have learned in experiencing and expressing peace, love, wisdom, happiness, and purpose.

This book was written so that the practice of prayer would help you toss out toxic thoughts, replace them with truth, and build into your daily life habits of trusting God and sharing what you have learned with others. Over the past weeks, you and the people close to you should have noticed a change in your attitude, affection, and actions. You have been transformed in the embrace of God, who has been pursuing you with all the peace, love, wisdom, happiness, and purpose that you have been searching for. You will need to continue to exercise these thoughts and practices daily to build strength and maintain a type of muscle memory that makes these habits a part of your everyday life and character.

Abide in prayer and God's Word, dwell in his presence and provision. Keep him in the forefront of your thoughts, and trust him in all circumstances. Let Jesus be your refuge from the enemy, and your fortress of power and authority so that you walk courageously and humbly through each day, fulfilling your purpose in his kingdom and knitting love through the lives you touch.

## INVITATION TO PRAYER

Lord, thank you for surrounding me with your presence. You are over and around me, the rock on which I stand and the wings that make me soar. I abide in you, dwelling in your protection and provision, obeying your commands, loving others, seeking justice, and making disciples. Thank you for supplying all that I need to do all that you ask. Your Spirit produces the fruit that is not only the noticeable change in my life but the charge that ignites my heart and hands to do your will. Let others take notice of all that you are doing in and through me so that they will want to abide in you, to be embraced by all that they are searching for.

# DAY 86

# MONDAY: PEACE

*Then justice will dwell in the wilderness,*
*and righteousness abide in the fruitful field.*
*And the effect of righteousness will be peace,*
*and the result of righteousness, quietness and trust forever.*
*My people will abide in a peaceful habitation,*
*in secure dwellings, and in quiet resting places.*

ISAIAH 32:16–18 ESV

As you abide in Christ, peace will abide in you. Being embraced by all that you need will feed the quiet security you have as you watch God's wondrous faithfulness throughout your life. Circumstances will not always turn out the way you want and planned, but you can rest assured that God will hold and control all of the moving parts that you cannot even see and that he will work everything out for kingdom good and purpose.

Abide in his kingdom; it is where your true citizenship resides. You are an ambassador on this earth, but you are formed in the image of God. He is your Father, and your eternal address is now and forever will be in his kingdom.

Take that in with a deep breath for a moment—maybe more. Feel peace fill you and let any distractions or worry flee as you sit still with your heavenly Father for a few more moments and tell him how much you love and appreciate him. Know that, just like any earthly relationship, God delights in spending focused time with you; you never bother him; you are not interrupting him; he is waiting to embrace you and hear about what is on your heart and what you did or need today; and he wants you to share about your friends, family, and neighbors. Tell him everything, linger in conversation as you abide in him continually. Inhabit his security and rest even as you work. Let righteousness be the character that causes you to think and act in wisdom and love. Rest in him as you resolve to think and act in the truth and fruit of the Holy Spirit. Let peace reside in you as you abide in Christ.

## INVITATION TO PRAYER

Lord, I just want to sit in your presence and praise you now. You are great and mighty, creator and counselor, wonderful and all-powerful. As I abide in you, I have all I need; I ascribe all of the blessings in my life to your wondrous works. Thank you for your peace that washes and watches over me.

# DAY 87

# TUESDAY: LOVE

*When I was a child, I spoke like a child, I thought like a child, I reasoned like a child. When I became a man, I gave up childish ways. For now we see in a mirror dimly, but then face to face. Now I know in part; then I shall know fully, even as I have been fully known. So now faith, hope, and love abide, these three; but the greatest of these is love.*

1 CORINTHIANS 13:11–13 ESV

As we grow up, we think and love differently. As we grow in Christ, as a branch abiding in the vine, his life-giving love flows and grows us. We can only see a piece, like a puzzle, of God's great picture. Limited by space, time, and flesh, we see what is in front and around us, but we cannot fully grasp the I Am who embraces us.

Faith, hope, and love are the lens we look through and the filter we live through, knowing that God's great love will provide as we abide. Faith strengthens and hope sustains, but love trains and shapes our view in all we go through and all we set our heart and hands to do through God's love. Our love reflects and responds to his love, because he loved us first and he loves us best.

When this world depletes us, we can come to Jesus empty and his love will fuel and fill us with all that we need to not only keep going, but to also keep sowing and growing. He is the potter who gently holds and molds us as the wheel and world spins round and round. Our love keeps us soft as we abide in his able hands. Purpose comes into focus, sometimes from a distance and sometimes close and clear, but in all we watch for his loving design and deeds and abide there in his care.

## INVITATION TO PRAYER

Loving God, there are many days and so many ways that I do not feel worthy of your love, yet before you spoke this world into existence, you loved me. Jesus, your love launched you from heaven's glory into the gospel story so that your example and expressions of love would remain throughout time as our model and mission. As I abide, God sees me through your blood and sees me wholly loved with holy love.

# DAY 88

# WEDNESDAY: WISDOM

*Let what you heard from the beginning abide in you.*
*If what you heard from the beginning abides in you,*
*then you too will abide in the Son and in the Father.*
*And this is the promise that he made to us—eternal life.*

1 JOHN 2:24–25 ESV

The wise review what they have learned so that it is not only a part of their character but also an immediate response, a pattern in the brain, a split-second decision. Wisdom abides in you as you abide in Christ. You have learned a lot over the past season through this book; look back and review previous lessons. If you are still struggling in a certain area, go back and work through that week again; as you review, you will see something new.

God's Word refreshes and is relevant for all that will be required of you each day. God has something to say about your relationships, decisions, work, money, family, and community, as well as your needs and the needs of those around you and around the world. God will reveal new wisdom even in places you feel strong, where he has given you opportunities to put wisdom into practice.

Throughout this book you were asked to take every thought captive and to inspect it to determine if it was truth or trash. If the thought was trash, you tossed it into the garbage and filled the space with new truth for meditation and motivation to live. Press forward and do not bring the trash back. You would never chase the garbage truck down the street to reclaim rotting food and soiled trash, so why would you even consider the foolishness of finding room for old habits and untruth? Let wisdom expand and erase any residue of foolishness that has tried to hide in the shadows. Let God's light shine so that good fruit can take root and prosper in you.

## INVITATION TO PRAYER

Lord, I want to abide in you—your Word, your presence, and your wisdom that is trustworthy and gives life. I want your wisdom to be my first thought, not something I take a long time weighing out; purify my mind so that your wisdom thrives in my thoughts. Let your Word wash away foolish worry, and forgiveness cleanse my conscience, so that wisdom has no rivals and no lie is revived as I abide in you.

# DAY 89

# THURSDAY: HAPPINESS

*As the Father has loved me, so have I loved you. Abide in my love. If you keep my commandments, you will abide in my love, just as I have kept my Father's commandments and abide in his love. These things I have spoken to you, that my joy may be in you, and that your joy may be full.*

JOHN 15:9–11 ESV

What greater happiness could there be than to abide in the love of God Almighty? Remember that we are happy because of our unchanging God, not hinged on changing circumstances and swinging moods. Remember that happiness is the precursor to success, and not the result of it.[23] Remember the *blessed* from the Sermon on the Mount ("happy are the …"), because God's economy of emotion is based on his goodness, not cultural perspectives and persuasions.

It is not willpower but God's power that enables you to shape the culture around you with your emotions. The Scripture and science go hand in hand as God whispers, "I told you so"—you can smile about that every time you think of it. As you abide in Christ and with other Christ followers, your happiness is increased. Isolation is the enemy's weapon, it steals your strength and destroys your happiness. Quiet times of rest are healthy, but isolation limits and eventually cripples us. Happy people take time, make time, to do things that they enjoy—laugh, interact with others, listen to music, exercise—but, whatever it is, always make God a part of it and don't do it apart from him.

You can influence a person's day and decisions with the emotion you share and spread. Happiness really is contagious and can cause a chain reaction that shapes the atmosphere of your home, school, and workplace. Stop to think of God's faithfulness, an answered prayer, or special blessings, and let it heap happiness into your life and help others.

## INVITATION TO PRAYER

Lord, you are *good!* I can smile, even sing, because you are worthy of my worship and the world should know of your great deeds in my life. You make the difference; the emotions you gave me must be filtered through your Spirit in me. I will decide to be happy as I abide in you.

# DAY 90

# FRIDAY: PURPOSE

*I am the vine; you are the branches. Whoever abides in me and I in him, he it is that bears much fruit, for apart from me you can do nothing.*

JOHN 15:5 ESV

As we wrap up this book, these are great parting truths I pray you will continually remember, reflect on, and respond to: Apart from God you can do nothing, but with him, nothing is impossible. You can do all things through Christ who strengthens you. As long as we continue to accept his invitation to prayer and abide in him, God will guide and provide all that we need for all that he requires in a lifestyle of intimacy with him.

God just asks for us to be willing; he does not force himself but knocks at the door of your heart he formed and the life he gave you so that you can gift it back to him. God says through the apostle Paul:

> "The God who made the world and all things in it, since He is Lord of heaven and earth, does not dwell in temples made with hands; nor is He

served by human hands, as though He needed anything, since He Himself gives to all people life and breath and all things; and He made from one man every nation of mankind to live on all the face of the earth, having determined their appointed times and the boundaries of their habitation, that they would seek God, if perhaps they might grope for Him and find Him, though He is not far from each one of us; for in Him we live and move and exist, as even some of your own poets have said, 'For we also are His children.'" (Acts 17:24–28)

## INVITATION TO PRAYER

God, you gave me life—right here, right now, with the people that surround me—for kingdom purposes on a kingdom timeline that stretches from everlasting to everlasting. I am not a mistake or a minor character in your story; I am deeply loved and sustained as I abide in you. Fear and worry have no place in my story. Doubt is cast out. Insecurity is a lie. You are never far and you never fail. In you I live and move in peace, love, wisdom, happiness, and purpose. I am made in your image, a child of God, part of a royal priesthood, set apart by your love, for love. Let this truth always abide in me as I abide in you, Christ Jesus my Lord.

# ENDNOTES

1    Sean Achor, *The Happiness Advantage: Seven Principles of Positive Psychology that Fuel Success and Performance at Work* (New York: Crown Publishing, 2010), 4.

2    Thayer and Smith, *The NAS New Testament Greek Lexicon* (1999), *s.v.* "makarios," accessed at Bible Study Tools, https://www.biblestudytools.com/lexicons/greek/nas/makarios.html.

3    Tom Popomaronis, "Science Says You Shouldn't Work More Than This Number of Hours a Week," *Inc*, May 9, 2016, https://www.inc.com/tom-popomaronis/science-says-you-shouldnt-work-more-than-this-number-of-hours-a-day.html.

4    "How Sleep Can Help You Be More Productive at Work," *Sleep.org*, National Sleep Foundation, https://sleep.org/articles/sleep-and-productivity-at-work/.

5    Dr. Caroline Leaf, *Switch on Your Brain: The Key to Peak Happiness, Thinking and Health* (Grand Rapids: Baker Books, 2013), 106.

6    Ibid., 107–108.

7    Dan Ohler, "How Does Neuroscience Affect Your Relationships?" *Thinkin' Outside the Barn* (blog), December 17, 2016, https://www.thinkinoutsidethebarn.com/how-does-neuroscience-affect-your-relationships/.

8    Liz Mineo, "Good Genes Are Nice, But Joy Is Better," *The Harvard Gazette*, April 11, 2017, https://news.harvard.edu/gazette/story/2017/04/over-nearly-80-years-harvard-study-has-been-showing-how-to-live-a-healthy-and-happy-life/.

9    Concordia University, "Feeling Bad Has Academic Benefits: Occasional Negative Moods Can Positively Impact Student Success," *ScienceDaily*, www.sciencedaily.com/releases/2016/11/161130131234.htm.

10    Mineo, "Good Genes Are Nice, but Joy Is Better."

11    Joshua Wolf Shenk, "What Makes Us Happy?" *Atlantic*, June 2009, https://www.theatlantic.com/magazine/archive/2009/06/what-makes-us-happy/307439/.

12    Brown, Driver, Briggs, and Gesenius, *The NAS Old Testament Hebrew Lexicon*, *s.v.* "towb," Bible Study Tools, https://www.biblestudytools.com/lexicons/hebrew/nas/towb.html.

13    Brown, Driver, Briggs, and Gesenius. *The NAS Old Testament Hebrew Lexicon*, *s.v.* "anah," Bible Study Tools, https://www.biblestudytools.com/lexicons/hebrew/nas/anah-4.html.

14    Eric Barker, "A Neuroscience Researcher Reveals Four Rituals That Will Make You Happier," *Business Insider*, September 26, 2015, https://www.businessinsider.com/a-neuroscience-researcher-reveals-4-rituals-that-will-make-you-a-happier-person-2015-9?r=UK&IR=T.

15    Thayer and Smith, *The NAS New Testament Greek Lexicon* (1999), *s.v.* "kardia," accessed at Bible Study Tools, https://www.biblestudytools.com/lexicons/greek/nas/kardia.html.

16    Niall McCarthy, "The Global Pyramid Of Wealth," *Statista*, November 2, 2015, https://www.statista.com/chart/3938/the-global-pyramid-of-wealth/.

17    Chris Weller, "A Neuroscientist Who Studies Decision-Making Reveals the Most Important Choice You Can Make," *Business Insider*, July 28, 2017, https://www.businessinsider.com/neuroscientist-most-important-choice-in-life-2017-7.

18    Lalin Anik and Michael I. Norton, "Matchmaking Promotes Happiness," *Social Psychological and Personality Science* 5, no. 6 (August 2014): 644, https://www.hbs.edu/faculty/Publication%20Files/Anik%20Norton%202014_69c76077-9dc5-43ef-a28e-cdbe968c892f.pdf.

19    Emma M. Seppälä, PhD, "Connect to Thrive: Social Connection Improves Health, Well-Being and Longevity," *Psychology Today*, August 26, 2012, https://www.psychologytoday.com/us/blog/feeling-it/201208/connect-thrive.

20    Achor, *The Happiness Advantage*, 14.

21    Daniel Goleman, "What Makes a Leader," in *Harvard Business Review 10 Must Reads* (Boston: Harvard Business School Publishing, 2015), 1.

22    Goleman, "What Makes a Leader," 13.

23    Achor, *The Happiness Advantage*, 3.

# About the Author

Kathy Branzell grew up in a military family that moved frequently and taught her to embrace a variety of people and places. This translated, in her Christian life, to a better understanding of how God calls us to love him and love our neighbors who are like ourselves, made in the image of God. Living in and visiting dozens of places gave Kathy the heart and mindset of worldwide neighbors and an appreciation for the likeness and differences that God designed in each of us. She loves to encourage people in their daily lives, prayer, and personal relationship with Jesus.

Kathy serves on the board of directors for the National Prayer Committee and The National Day of Prayer, where she assists in the areas of philanthropy and partnerships in addition to traveling across America with the National Day of Prayer on their "Pray for America" bus tours. She also serves as the director of partnerships and philanthropy for the National Day of Prayer.

Kathy is the national coordinator of LOVE2020 and is a longtime member of Mission America Coalition, now known as the Table Coalition.

She is the author of other BroadStreet Publishing books, including *An Apple a Day: 365 Devotionals for Educators* and *40 Days of Love: A Prayer-Care-Share Devotional.*

Kathy earned her bachelor's degree in education from the University of Georgia and went on to earn a master's degree in biblical studies from Liberty Theological Seminary.

She is the wife to her childhood sweetheart, Russ, and mom to their son, Chandler, and daughter, Emily.